MODERN WORLD NATIONS

WITHDRAWN

MODERN WORLD NATIONS

# Democratic Republic of the Congo

Joseph R. Oppong

and

Tania Woodruff

Series Editor
**Charles F. Gritzner**
South Dakota State University

**CHELSEA HOUSE**
P U B L I S H E R S

An Imprint of Infobase Publishing

*Frontispiece:* Flag of the Democratic Republic of the Congo

*Cover:* A village in the Democratic Republic of the Congo

**Democratic Republic of the Congo**

Copyright © 2007 by Infobase Publishing

Chelsea House
An imprint of Infobase Publishing
132 West 31st Street
New York NY 10001

ISBN-10: 0-7910-9249-6
ISBN-13: 978-0-7910-9249-1

**Library of Congress Cataloging-in-Publication Data**

Oppong, Joseph R.
  Democratic Republic of the Congo / Joseph R. Oppong and Tania Woodruff.
    p. cm.—(Modern world nations)
  Includes bibliographical references and index.
  Audience: Grades 9-12.
  ISBN 0-7910-9249-6 (hardcover)
  1. Congo (Democratic Republic)—Juvenile literature. I. Woodruff, Tania. II. Title. III. Series.

  DT644.O67 2007
  967.51—dc22

2006032008

Chelsea House books are available at special discounts when purchased in bulk quantities for businesses, associations, institutions, or sales promotions. Please call our Special Sales Department in New York at (212) 967-8800 or (800) 322-8755.

You can find Chelsea House on the World Wide Web at http://www.chelseahouse.com

Series and cover design by Takeshi Takahashi

Printed in the United States of America

Bang Hermitage 10 9 8 7 6 5 4 3 2 1

This book is printed on acid-free paper.

All links, Web addresses, and Internet search terms were checked and verified to be correct at the time of publication. Because of the dynamic nature of the Web, some addresses and links may have changed since publication and may no longer be valid.

# Table of Contents

# Democratic Republic of the Congo

# CHAPTER

# 1

# Introducing the Democratic Republic of the Congo

I magine a country that is rich in valuable natural resources such as gold, diamonds, and oil. Much of its area is covered by dense forests and wildlife abounds. Africa's second-longest river cascades down steep terrain, creating perhaps 20 percent of the entire world's hydroelectric potential. It has varied terrain, ranging from broad basins to spectacular snowcapped mountains. The country has a long human history and is home to a variety of peoples. It is a fascinating land of striking natural beauty and diverse cultures.

Yet despite these many apparent advantages, this huge and heavily populated country is very poor. In fact, it is one of the world's poorest countries. Its per-capita income and gross national product

Much of the Democratic Republic of the Congo is covered by the world's second-largest rain forest (after South America's Amazon). Pictured here is the lush Nouabalé-Ndoki National Park, which was established in 1993 to preserve more than 1,622 square miles (4,200 square kilometers) of this unique habitat.

both rank at or near the very bottom among nations. Few places in the world can come close to matching the day-to-day conditions experienced by most of this country's residents. The Human Development Index, a ranking of countries using a number of factors that measure human well-being, ranks this country close to the bottom of the list. It is often suggested that the country is on a "life-support system"; that it struggles to function only with generous support from the United Nations and other donor agencies. In fact, the UN and its organizations are the glue and Band-Aid that hold this country together in an attempt to stop further hemorrhaging. Many observers wonder how long it will be able to survive. What led to this situation? Why are the residents of such a large country, which has the potential to become an economic giant, on its knees begging for help? How long can it survive without major changes in its present course? Indeed, will it survive? Welcome to the Democratic Republic of the Congo (DRC), a country of extreme paradoxes!

This book tells the story of the Democratic Republic of the Congo. It is the story of a nation with an abundance of resources, but its people are not prosperous; they are languishing in heartbreaking poverty. Much of the blame for the country's current sad state can be attributed to early colonial exploitation. More recently, the wanton greed and jealousy of neighboring countries have produced what has been called Africa's "World War." Since 1997, the country has experienced two deadly wars. These bitter conflicts involved seven foreign armies, were responsible for the deaths of at least 4 million people, and left widespread abuse, disease, and destruction in their wake. This is the story of the Congolese. Culturally, they are a desperate people torn apart by language and ethnic divisions. Physically, they struggle with natural environmental hazards such as earthquakes and diseases. As citizens of one of the world's poorest countries, they remain almost helpless as neighboring countries fight to plunder their natural wealth. In 2006, an estimated 38,000 people were dying each month from easily treatable conditions such as diarrhea and respiratory infections.

The focus of this book is on the physical, historical, and human geography of this beautiful, yet troubled, country. You will better understand how its geographic location has contributed to these problems—how its relative location places it at risk. You will understand how and why internal divisions and ethnic strife almost always produce poverty and destitution. You will also meet children, some of whom may be your age, and hear the stories of their lives as child soldiers. In this book, you will explore the fascinating world of geography—how and why things are located where they are, and why their location is important. Are you ready for a life-changing journey into the very heart of Africa?

The Democratic Republic of the Congo (DRC) is located in Central Africa. It is a huge country, the third largest on the African continent (only Sudan and Algeria are larger in area). With an area of 905,585 square miles (2,345,410 square kilometers), the DRC is larger than Texas and Alaska combined! In fact, the country is about one-quarter the size of the United States. To cite an example from Europe, DRC is larger than France, Germany, Spain, Denmark, the Netherlands, Belgium, Switzerland, Austria, and the United Kingdom combined. It shares boundaries with nine neighboring countries. Moving clockwise beginning in the southwest, the DRC borders Angola, Republic of Congo, Central African Republic, Sudan, Uganda, Rwanda, Burundi, Tanzania, and Zambia.

The country's total population is about 60 million, nearly twice as many people as live in all of Canada, or in California, the leading U.S. state in population. But the population is hardly homogeneous. In fact, there are many different tribal and ethnic groups that speak an estimated 242 different languages. This cultural diversity is one of the primary reasons for the country's ongoing political instability. Language can be both a centrifugal and a centripetal force. A centrifugal force divides people, or forces them apart, whereas a centripetal force unites them. People are usually drawn together if they share a common language, religion, and other cultural institutions. In contrast, religious and ethnic differences, as well as language barriers, promote division as they produce rivalries and jealousies. Thus, with but few exceptions, countries with multiple

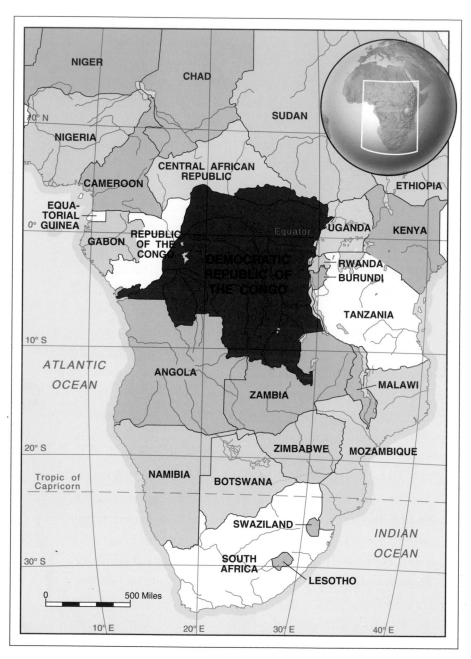

Located in Central Africa, the Democratic Republic of the Congo shares borders with nine countries: Angola, Republic of Congo, Central African Republic, Sudan, Uganda, Rwanda, Burundi, Tanzania, and Zambia. The DRC is Africa's third-largest country (905,585 square miles, 2,345,410 square kilometers) and is greater in size than Texas and Alaska combined.

languages and ethnic groups tend to be less stable than those that are united by language, religion, and ethnicity.

To counter the divisive influence of multiple languages, many countries frequently choose an official language, the tongue used for official government business. It is meant to be an ethnically neutral language that allows easy communication and also unites the diverse ethnic groups. In the DRC, the official language adopted at independence was French. Since then, four major languages—Lingala, Kikongo, Tshiluba, and Swahili—also have been elevated to the status of official national languages. This diversity of tongues, of course, adds to the divisions among peoples and regions of the country.

The Democratic Republic of the Congo straddles the equator and sits at the very center of the African continent. Few countries in the world can match its mineral wealth. The DRC has rich deposits of gold, silver, and diamonds; industrial metals include cobalt, copper, zinc, manganese, and tin; and energy sources include petroleum, coal, and uranium. It also has an abundance of other natural resources such as hydroelectric potential and timber. More than half of Africa's tropical rain forest ecosystem is found in this country. In fact, Africa is home to the world's second-largest rain forest, surpassed in area only by the vast rain forest that spans much of South America's Amazon Basin. The forest covers much of the country. In addition, the DRC is home to a number of rare and endangered animal species such as forest elephants, Congo peacocks, and gorillas. Yet, the country's own citizens have ravaged this beautiful physical environment, as they desperately try to make a living amidst the surrounding chaos. As a result, the DRC faces problems of deforestation, water pollution, poaching of its wildlife, and stripping away of its mineral resources.

In order to understand the Democratic Republic of the Congo, we must look back over time and consider the country's historical geography. What is today the DRC was first established in 1908 as a Belgian trading colony. It was included as a parcel in what at the time was known as the Middle Congo. Upon gaining its independence in 1960, the country became the Republic of the Congo, but neither peace nor the name lasted for long. In November 1965, Colonel Joseph Mobutu seized power and declared himself president. In celebration of the occasion, not only did he change his own name to Mobutu Sese Seko, but he changed the name of the country as well, to Zaire. After governing for 32 years as an often ruthless dictator, the Mobutu regime was toppled by Laurent Kabila who, in 1997, again renamed the country—this time as the Democratic Republic of the Congo (DRC). Kabila's government did not last long. In August 1998, a group of rebels backed by the countries of Rwanda and Uganda challenged his regime. But military forces from Angola, Zimbabwe, Namibia, Chad, and Sudan intervened in support of Kabila. In January 2001, Laurent Désiré Kabila was assassinated and his son Joseph was named head of state. In December 2002, the Pretoria Accord was signed by all remaining warring parties to establish a peaceful government. Its leaders include President Kabila and vice presidents representing the former government, former rebel troops, and the political opposition.

That is quite a bloody history, don't you think? But that certainly is not the end of the chaotic story! Fighting goes on today, particularly in the eastern part of the country, where foreign armies continue to plunder the vast mineral wealth. The war has destabilized the economy by disrupting normal economic activities. The country also faces the threat of a serious AIDS epidemic. An estimated 1.1 million of the 60 million citizens of the Democratic Republic of the Congo currently live with HIV/AIDS. Diseases such as hepatitis, typhoid fever, malaria, plague, and African sleeping sickness also are rampant. Contributing to their spread are dreadfully poor sanitation, disrupted health services, and other adverse conditions that are created or worsened by war. Children, in particular, are traumatized by war. Schools are closed, food is scarce, and sometimes they are even forced to fight.

Why is there so much conflict in this nation? Why are certain diseases worse here than in other parts of the world? How can a country be so rich in natural resources and so poor economically? It is questions such as these that geographers attempt to answer. Geography is concerned with where things are, why they are there, and how they are important. Geographers can study anything on Earth's surface. They are interested in physical geography, that branch of the science that involves natural land features such as volcanoes, mountains, and valleys. The weather and climate of an area—whether it is hot or cold, wet or dry, calm or stormy—also is a very important aspect of physical geography. So, too, is knowledge of an area's ecosystems, the types of natural vegetation, animal life, soils, water features, and mineral resources that it offers. Geographers try to understand how each of these elements comes together in a particular place. They also want to know how people culturally adapt to, use, and modify the natural environments in which they live.

Geographers are not only concerned with the physical aspects of a place. They also study how humans live in their environment. This is important because the way people interact with their environment varies from place to place. For example, in a similar natural setting, some people may depend on hunting animals and gathering the plants that grow naturally, whereas others will practice various types of agriculture. Still others may use the environment in ways totally different, such as mining mineral resources, or using nature's wonders to attract tourists to the area. Geographers study all aspects of a society, from the location and layout of cities to rural farming practices. They are particularly interested in population, settlement, economic activity, and political organizations. But they also study languages, religions, social patterns and practices, customs, and diets. In essence, geographers attempt to understand and explain why the ways in which people live vary so much from place to place. This is called *human* (or *cultural*) geography.

In addition to studying the physical aspects of a region, geographers also study the way people in that region interact with their environment. For example, fishing is an important cultural trait of the Wagenia people, who reside near Kisangani (formerly Stanleyville). Here, a boy straddles a wooden pole, which the Wagenias use to hang their fishing nets from.

The ways in which the answers to these questions come together is what makes each country unique, and the Democratic Republic of the Congo is certainly unique! With its history of warfare and strife, the nation appears to be an unpleasant place, right? But that is only one aspect of this intriguing country, which is full of dark and mysterious rain forests, beautiful beaches, and dazzling mountain views.

# 2

# Physical Landscapes

D o you live in a somewhat boring physical environment? For example, is your home surrounded by plains or mountains, or all forest, or perhaps prairie grassland? Do you prefer a landscape that offers a variety of features and conditions? If so, then you will enjoy exploring the Democratic Republic of the Congo. There are vast expanses of tropical rain forest with its massive trees; there are areas of savanna grassland, home to many of Africa's prized "big game" animals; and there are even towering snowcapped mountains. Let us take time and explore the physical geography of this remarkably diverse country that sits astride the equator.

The Democratic Republic of the Congo (DRC) is a land of spectacular beauty and varied physical landscapes. It does have one major disadvantage: The country is all but landlocked with only a very short 25-mile (40-kilometer) coastline facing the Atlantic Ocean. Elevation varies from sea level along the Atlantic coastline to the Ruwenzori

Mountain range, which rises to an elevation of 16,761 feet (5,109 meters) and is permanently capped with snow. Only two other permanently snowcapped mountains exist on the continent. They are Tanzania's Mount Kilimanjaro, Africa's highest peak with an elevation of 19,340 feet (5,895 meters), and Mount Kenya in Kenya, which reaches a height of 17,058 feet (5,199 meters). Between the narrow coastal plain and the eastern mountains, much of the Congo is covered by plateaus. In the eastern Great Rift Valley, however, there are even volcanoes. Vegetation also varies greatly. There are vast expanses of tropical rain forest and large areas of tropical savanna. On mountain slopes, vegetation changes rapidly with elevation. In fact, one can literally pass from dense tropical forest conditions to polar tundra vegetation within a few short (horizontal) miles!

Yes, there is snow in Africa, even near the equator! Temperatures generally decline with increasing altitude. Thus, areas with higher elevations can have very low temperatures that make snowfall possible. Next time you travel to Colorado or some other place with high elevations, remember to bring some warm clothes, because you could get very cold.

## LAND FEATURES

Geographers identify areas with similar features or characteristics as *regions*. This concept is very handy for characterizing the physical diversity of the DRC. The huge country can be divided into four major regions based on their unique physical characteristics. These are the Congo River Basin, Northern Uplands, Southern Uplands, and the Eastern Highlands. Most of the country lies in the Congo River Basin. This region is made up primarily of tropical rain forest, with a mixture of swamp, marshes, and firm land. The basin has the shape of an amphitheater, open to the north and northwest and closed in the south and east by high plateaus and mountains. The edges of the basin are breached in the west by the Congo River as it passes to the Atlantic Ocean.

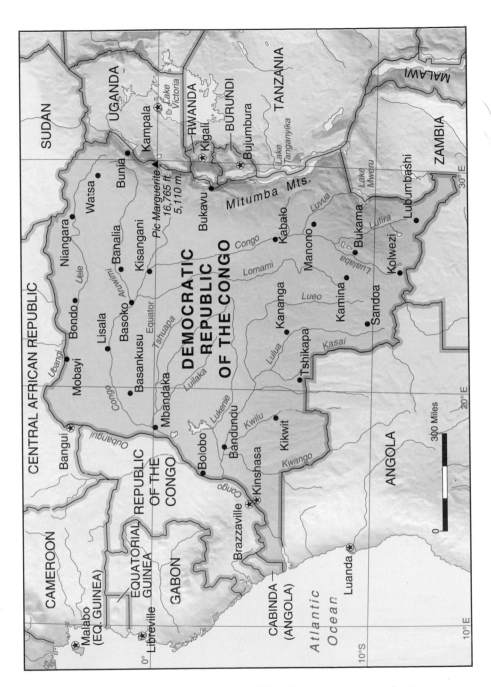

The Democratic Republic of the Congo is divided into four regions: the Congo River Basin, Northern Uplands, Southern Uplands, and Eastern Highlands. The country's highest point, Pic Marguerite, is located in the eastern part of the country, near the border with Uganda.

North and south of the Congo River Basin are the North-ern Uplands and Southern Uplands. These are mainly hills covered with savanna grasses and scattered woodlands. The Southern Uplands region covers about a third of Congo's territory. The area slopes downward in elevation from south to north. Vegetation cover varies more in the Southern Uplands than the Northern Uplands. In some areas, woodland is dominant; in others, savanna grasses and scattered woodlands predominate. South of the basin, along the streams flowing into the Kasai River, are extensive forests. In the far southeast, somewhat higher plateaus and low mountains characterize most of the Shaba region. The westernmost section of Congo, a partly forested panhandle reaching the Atlantic Ocean, is an extension of the Southern Uplands. Near the coast, it drops sharply as the plateau escarpment (steep slope) plunges toward a very narrow shoreline and coastal plain.

The Eastern Highlands region is the highest and most rugged portion of the country. It is also the most spectacular. Highlands extend for more than 900 miles (1,500 kilometers) and cover the entire eastern flank of the DRC from north of Lake Albert southward to the town of Lubumbashi. The western arm of the Great Rift Valley forms a natural eastern boundary to this region. It extends through the Great Rift Valley and its system of long, deep lakes. In this region, changes in elevation bring marked changes in vegetation, which ranges from upland savanna to heavily forested mountain slopes. The height and location of these mountains on the equator contribute to a varied and spectacular amount of plant life. The area around Lake Kivu (site of several active volcanoes) and the Virunga Mountains (in the western part of the country), and the game park situated between them, constitutes Congo's most important potential tourist resource.

## WEATHER AND CLIMATE

Like its terrain, Congo's weather (daily conditions) and climate (long-term average weather) are extremely varied. Two primary factors influence the country's weather and climate: its equatorial location and differences in elevation. DRC lies astride the equator, with one-third of the country's area located to the north and two-thirds to the south. This distribution results in the northern part of the country experiencing summer, while the southern part is in the middle of "winter." When a country is so close to the equator, however, there isn't a whole lot of difference between winter and summer! Thus, elevation is much more important than seasons in determining weather conditions and temperature differences throughout the Congo. South of the equator, the rainy season lasts from October to May; north of the equator, it is from April to November. Along the equator, rainfall is fairly regular throughout the year.

The wet season brings frequent, violent thunderstorms that seldom last more than a few hours. The average annual rainfall for the entire country is about 42 inches (107 centimeters). There is a great deal of variation, however, with some locations receiving as much as 100 inches (250 centimeters) of precipitation annually. Annual rainfall is highest in the heart of the Congo River Basin and in the highlands west of Bukavu. With some variations, precipitation tends to diminish in direct relation to distance from these areas. The only areas marked by long four- to five-month dry seasons and occasional droughts are parts of the southern Shaba region. With seasons in opposition, most places away from the equator on either side experience two wetter or two drier seasons.

In general, temperatures and humidity are quite high in the Congo. Equatorial areas, in general, experience the world's highest *annual average* temperatures. In the DRC, the average annual temperature varies from about 77°F to 81°F (25° to 27° C). Surprisingly, perhaps, areas near the equator do not experience the highest *extreme* temperatures. In fact, higher temperatures have been recorded north of the Arctic Circle than have ever occurred in the humid tropics! In the DRC, the highest and least variable temperatures occur in the equatorial forest region. There, daytime high temperatures range between 86°F (30°C) and 95°F (35°C) and nighttime lows rarely drop below 68°F (20°C). In the Southern Uplands, particularly in southeastern Shaba, winters are cool and dry, whereas summers are warm and damp. The area embracing the chain of lakes from Lake Albert to Lake Tanganyika in the Eastern Highlands has a moist climate and a narrow but not excessively warm temperature range. The mountain sections are cooler, but humidity increases with elevation until the saturation point is reached. As a result, a nearly constant falling mist prevails on some slopes, particularly in the Ruwenzori Mountains, just like it does in Seattle, Washington, or Victoria, British Columbia.

## WATER BODIES

The Congo River and its tributaries (including the Kasai, Ubangi, Aruwimi, and Lulonga) form the backbone for Congolese transportation and its economy. The mighty stream originates in the mountains and highlands surrounding the East African Rift Valley region, as well as in Lake Tanganyika and Lake Mweru. It has the second-largest flow and the second-largest watershed of any river in the world, exceeded only by South America's huge Amazon. Its flow is unusually regular, because rivers and streams feed it from both north and south of the equator. The complementary alternation of rainy and dry seasons on each side of the equator guarantees a regular supply of water for the main channel. At points where rapids and waterfalls block navigation, the sudden descent of the river creates a hydroelectric potential greater than that found in any other river system on Earth.

Most of Congo's lakes are also part of the Congo River Basin. In the west are Lake Mai-Ndombe and Lake Tumba. These water bodies are remnants of a huge interior lake that once occupied the entire basin. Eventually, however, the edge of the basin was breached by the Congo River, resulting in the lake being partially drained. In the southeast, Lake Mweru straddles

Stretching some 2,720 miles (4,375 kilometers), the Congo is the second-longest river in Africa (behind the Nile). The lower part of the river (near Kinshasa, in the southwestern part of the country) is largely unnavigable due to rapids such as the ones pictured here.

the border with Zambia. On the eastern frontier, Lake Kivu, Central Africa's highest lake, and Lake Tanganyika to the immediate south, both feed into the Lualaba River (as the upper Congo often is called). Only waters of the northernmost great lakes on the eastern frontier, Edward and Albert, drain northward into the drainage basin of the Nile River.

With a length of 420 miles (673 kilometers) and depth of 4,710 feet (1,436 meters), Lake Tanganyika is the longest and second-deepest freshwater body in the world. (Lake Baikal in Siberia reaches a depth of 5,371 feet, or 1,637 meters.) It also holds the greatest volume of freshwater. In surface area, however, it is only the second-largest lake in Africa (trailing Lake Victoria, which is exceeded in area only by North America's Lake Superior). The lake is situated within the western rift of the Great Rift Valley and is confined by the steep escarpments of the valley. The lake is divided among four countries: Burundi, Democratic Republic of the Congo, Tanzania, and Zambia. Nearly half of the water body lies within the DRC.

## EARTHQUAKES AND VOLCANOES

Have you ever seen a volcano erupt or felt the jolt of an earthquake? You may experience both of these environmental hazards in the Democratic Republic of the Congo. Clarisse and Chance, both 10 years old, are on their way to school. They live in Goma. In the last two weeks, they have heard and felt mild earth tremors every day, particularly at night. They fear that Mount Nyiragongo, a volcanic peak towering over the town of Goma, could erupt again at any time. Wearing flip-flops, they clamber over a 1,600-foot (500-meter) stretch of lava left from the last eruption.

During the volcanic eruption in 2002, Goma became a divided city with a "Berlin Wall" made from the black volcanic lava that poured out of Mount Nyiragongo and spewed into the heart of the city's commercial district. Clarisse lost her home beneath the searing hot lava during the eruption. The UN estimates that at least 300 buildings, or about 40 percent of the entire town, were destroyed by the lava flow from the eruption in 2002. Tens of thousands of people became homeless in Goma and surrounding areas. Several of Clarisse's friends and classmates were killed. Her father lost his job as a driver. Now, the family of seven lives on the edge of town in a tiny tent made from scraps of plastic sheeting, sticks, old lumps of lava, and banana leaves. Clarisse's school was destroyed, too, but it has been rebuilt.

Clarisse and Chance walk past two older boys, Fiston Mirind and Joseph Makelele. "The eruption was bad," says 14-year-old Joseph. "But the war is much worse. I've lost my whole family because of it." After his parents were shot by soldiers, Joseph lived on the street for two years. Now, he is happy to be in school, but he is also concerned that another eruption will occur. Clarisse and Chance wonder which is worse—the seemingly never-ending war or the omnipresent threat of another volcanic eruption.

Where do volcanoes come from? Why do they occur in some places and not in others? Deep within the earth, it is so hot that some rocks slowly melt and become a thick flowing substance called *magma*. Because it is lighter than the solid rock around it, magma rises and collects in chambers deep inside the earth. Eventually, some of the magma pushes through vents and fissures in Earth's surface resulting in a volcanic eruption. Magma that reaches the surface is called *lava*.

Some volcanic eruptions are explosive and others are not. Explosive volcanic eruptions (as occurred with the 1980 eruption of Mount St. Helen's in Washington State) can be dangerous and deadly. Lava flows, however, rarely kill people. Their movement is slow enough for people to get out of their way. Nonetheless, lava flows can cause considerable destruction to buildings in their path. Nyiragongo eruptions are extremely hazardous, because the lava tends to be very fluid, allowing it to pour down the volcano's slopes very quickly. The lava flow that destroyed Clarisse's home was about 6 feet (about 2 meters) high and moved at an alarming speed of about 60 miles (100 kilometers) per hour. Eruptions can be large and spectacular, and flows can reach up to 10 or more miles (tens of kilometers) from the volcano very quickly. Also, biomass burned from Nyriagongo eruptions, and those of nearby Mount Nyamuragira, tends to create clouds of smoke. The smoke, in turn, adversely affects both people and wildlife, including the increasingly rare mountain gorillas that inhabit the adjacent mountain chain.

## THE GREAT RIFT VALLEY

Before leaving Congo's physical geography behind, we must visit the Great Rift Valley. This huge crack (rift) in Earth's surface is truly one of the world's greatest and most scenic

Located in the eastern part of the Democratic Republic of the Congo, Mount Nyiragongo has erupted 15 times since 1883, most recently in 2006. The town of Goma has repeatedly been affected by these eruptions; the worst of which came in 2002, which is when this photo was taken.

natural wonders. It extends nearly 2,000 miles (3,200 kilometers), has an average width of 30 to 40 miles (50 to 65 kilometers), and is bordered by steep escarpments that rise abruptly from the valley floor. Faulting has occurred here for millions of years and continues today, breaking apart the African continent. Faults happen between two parts of Earth's crust that are moving slowly and sporadically in relation to each other. Movement can be in any direction—up, down, or horizontally. When two pieces of land are being pulled apart, numerous parallel faults develop between them as the edges break off and are forced downward. The resulting formation is known as a rift valley, with a steadily lowering valley floor bounded by steep cliffs known as rift escarpments. The Great Rift Valley system of East Africa traces sets of parallel faults in the African Plate that run from the Afar Depression in Eritrea (formally part of Ethiopia) and Djibouti to southern Mozambique. Millions of years from now, as the Great Rift Valley continues to widen and deepen, East Africa will likely split off from the continent. When this happens, all of Africa east of the Great Rift Valley will become the world's largest island!

Rifting of the continent in this area also has shown itself in the famous great lakes of East Africa that lie on the Congo's eastern frontier. The DRC is bordered in the east by two of these: Lake Albert and Lake Tanganyika. Perhaps most important of all, the rift valley has endowed most of the southern and eastern margins of the DRC with an enormous amount of mineral wealth. Unfortunately, this wealth has been more of a curse than a blessing. From ancient times, it has always been a source of conflict, or reason for exploitation and enslavement, of the Congolese. This mineral wealth is a primary reason for the recent war that has decimated the country—neighbors have taken advantage of chaos to pillage Congo's rich store of minerals.

## PLANT AND ANIMAL LIFE

Congo is home to a spectacular variety of flora (plants) and fauna (animals). Tropical rain forest dominates the country's ecosystem. Rain forests are incredibly diverse, supporting up to 2,500 species of trees alone in the Congo. Trees form three separate layers. The tallest may grow to heights of 150 to 200 feet (45 to 60 meters). A second tier reaches an average height of 80 to 120 feet (25 to 35 meters) when mature, and a third, lower group matures to heights of about 40 to 60 feet (12 to 18 meters). Combined, their crowns create a dense overhead canopy that blocks most if not all of the sunlight. The forest floor is a dark and eerie green, and little photosynthesis (which is essential to plant growth) occurs. As a result, very few plants can survive at ground level, leaving a relatively clear surface. Where, then, does this leave room for the widely held perception that a "jungle" is a dense, almost impenetrable tangle of vegetation? True jungle can only occur where sunlight reaches the forest floor. These conditions exist on the borders of roadways, streams, agricultural clearings, and villages—the only environments experienced by most visitors! This reality tends to reinforce the notion that rain forest and jungle are one and the same. But they are not. In fact, only about 1 percent of the rain forest ecosystem supports a true jungle cover.

Rain forests contain great biodiversity, including many rare, native species. Examples include the common chimpanzee and the bonobo (also known as the pygmy chimpanzee), mountain gorilla, okapi (a strange looking cousin to the giraffe), and white rhino. Five of the country's national parks are listed as World Heritage Sites by the United Nations Educational, Scientific and Cultural Organization (UNESCO). They include Garamba National Park in the Northeast, Kahuzi-Biega National Park in the Eastern Lowlands, Salonga National Park in the heart of the rain forest, Virunga National Park on the border with Rwanda, and the Okapi Wildlife Reserve in the Ituri Forest of northeastern DRC.

Perhaps the best known of Africa's ecosystems is the savanna, that vast area of grasslands and scattered trees that borders the rain forest in both hemispheres. Both the northern and southern areas of the DRC fall within this zone of tall grass savanna. This environment is famous (in Africa) for its abundant wildlife—Africa's famous "big game" animals. Unfortunately, few tourists dare venture into this war-torn region for fear that they themselves might become the quarry. Should conditions within the DRC eventually stabilize, tourism does hold considerable potential if the necessary infrastructure can be developed.

Bonobos, also known as pygmy chimpanzees, are an endangered species that are only found in the Democratic Republic of the Congo. Over the last 25 years, the number of bonobos has declined significantly: from 100,000 in 1980 to less than 10,000 today. Pictured here are several bonobos at the Lola Ya Bonobo Sanctuary near Kinshasa.

## ENVIRONMENTAL ISSUES

Unfortunately, the civil war (which has been ongoing since 1994) and resultant poor economic conditions have endangered much of the Congo's biodiversity. Refugees from neighboring Angola, Rwanda, Sudan, and Uganda are partly responsible for significant deforestation, soil erosion, and wildlife poaching. In fact, all five World Heritage Sites are listed by UNESCO as World Heritage in Danger. Rebel troops are using these national parks as bases, and killing both protected animal species and park rangers. Consequently, many park wardens have either fled or been killed. (Between 1996 and 2006, it is estimated that about one of every seven park rangers was murdered on the job!)

For the past 10 years, loggers have besieged Congo's vast tropical rain forest. About 37 percent of the total forested area is designated as holding timber to be logged. The most intense logging to date has been in the Bas-Zaïre region in the hinterlands of the capital, Kinshasa. Cutting down trees disrupts the forest ecology. Logging roads permit poor farmers to enter the forest, clearing and burning more trees to make fields for their crops. Should the rich natural diversity be preserved for future generations while people are hungry for land and food today? This poses a real dilemma for the Congolese. What do you think?

Another huge environmental concern is poaching and the hunger for "bushmeat." Bushmeat is the meat of wild animals. Typically, it is obtained by trapping, usually with wire snares set by hunters; increasingly, however, guns originally intended for use in the DRC's numerous military conflicts are used to shoot game. A rapidly growing population and deplorable economic conditions have forced many Congolese to depend on bushmeat for food or as a means of acquiring income (hunting and selling the meat). Major cities such as Kinshasa are the prime market for bushmeat. This practice, while providing much-needed food, is taking a terrible toll on wildlife, including a number of endangered species.

Besides depleting the beautiful wildlife, there is one other important reason why the bushmeat market is dangerous. Humans are susceptible to many of the same diseases that affect chimpanzees, bonobos, gorillas, and orangutans. Historically, there was little contact between people and these apes, so little opportunity existed for diseases to transfer between species. Increased population growth, human migration, and access to forest habitats have now exposed humans to diseases carried by these animals. For example, scientists have linked the first human cases of Ebola to the handling of meat from infected apes. Discovered in 1976, the Ebola virus is fatal to both apes and humans in a high proportion of cases.

Recent outbreaks have killed hundreds of people and thousands of apes in the Congo. Similarly, scientists suspect that humans first acquired HIV/AIDS through direct exposure to animal blood and secretions during hunting, butchering, or consumption of uncooked contaminated meat. Risk of disease transmission is a strong argument against the consumption of primate bushmeat.

Our tour of the vast and varied physical geography of Congo is now complete. What do you think of the country so far? Well, don't get too comfortable, because our journey is far from over! We can now turn our attention to the country's equally varied and tumultuous history.

# 3

# The Congo Through Time

L
ong, long ago, Pygmies were the only inhabitants of the Congo. These dark-skinned hunting and gathering people, who live in equatorial rain forests, average less than five feet (150 centimeters) in height. Later, Bantu-speaking people migrated into the area from the northwest (present-day Nigeria and Cameroon) and settled in the savanna regions of the south. By about 2000 B.C., the Bantu tribes had displaced the indigenous Pygmy population, forcing their tiny neighbors yet deeper into the dark rain forest. The knowledge of iron technology and agriculture, which came with the Bantu, quickly diffused to other parts of the Congo and elsewhere in Africa. From about A.D. 700, the Bantu worked the copper deposits of Katanga and traded over wide areas.

Since this early Bantu invasion, the Democratic Republic of the Congo has experienced an almost-constant flow of other people and cultures into the region. Migrants arrived from many different places, including the Darfur and Kordofan regions of Sudan, and other parts of East Africa. This added to the mix of ethnic groups in the DRC. In this chapter, you will explore the major kingdoms that shaped the present-day nation and learn why it has always been a land of civil unrest.

## PRE-EUROPEAN CONGO

The Kongo Kingdom (from which the name Congo was derived) began as a number of small Iron Age communities lying just north of the River Congo (formerly Zaire River). This strategic location provided fertile soil, iron and copper ore, a rich source of fish, and a river that was navigable upstream for more than 2,000 miles (3,200 kilometers). By the early fifteenth century, these communities had grown in wealth and size to form a loose federation centered on one kingdom, led by a king, or Manikongo. Common goods produced in the Kongo included metal work, pottery, and raffia textiles (a fiber made from the leaves of an African palm).

The Kongo expanded less through military conquest than it did through trade, alliances, and marriages. The Manikongo exercised sovereignty through governors. For example, when increased population density created demand for new food supplies, he chose several chiefs to lead expeditions in search of new territory. They set off in all directions and established new outposts to the Kongo Empire. Thus, at its height, Kongo was the biggest state in western Central Africa. It stretched from the Atlantic Ocean in the west to the Kwango River in the east, including what is today northern Angola and parts of the DRC and the Republic of the Congo. By the fifteenth century, the dominant political force of the Congo region was the Kongo Empire. It had developed an intricate system of taxation and was the hub of an extensive Central African trade network based on slaves and natural resources.

Numerous other, although much smaller, states emerged throughout the region. For example, along the banks of the Lualaba River in the modern-day Katanga province, the Upemba emerged and eventually evolved into the Luba Kingdom. The Luba established a strong commercial demand for metal technologies. They also developed a primitive but long-range commercial network that stretched all the way to the Indian Ocean. By the 1500s, the kingdom had established a strong central government based on chieftainship.

The Kuba Kingdom was a federation of approximately 20 Bantu ethnic groups that emerged in southern Congo. It covered some 40,000 square miles (100,000 square kilometers) and had a population of approximately 150,000 inhabitants. Due to its relative remoteness, Kuba escaped most of the turmoil of both the European and Afro-Arab slave trade. As a result, the civilization was able to maintain itself until the nineteenth century. Even after Belgium officially established the Congo Free State in the 1880s, the Kubas were able to sustain their federation.

Before the arrival of the Portuguese in the late fifteenth century, slavery was already established in the Congo. Most slaves were war captives, criminals, or debtors who could eventually earn back their freedom. Arab nations were the major traders and captured persons were typically shipped to the Middle East for labor. After Europeans arrived, clan chiefs and African Muslim slave traders began to sell their slaves to the Portuguese and other Europeans, who transported them to America. This slave trading gradually depopulated and weakened the once-powerful Kingdom of the Kongo.

## EUROPEAN EXPLORATION OF THE CONGO

In the mid-1800s, central Africa remained one of the few areas of the African continent not colonized by any European power. Beginning in 1871, American journalist Henry M. Stanley led an expedition that reached the headwaters of the Congo River, and finally reached the shores of the Atlantic Ocean in 1877.

His travels spanned some 7,000 miles (11,300 kilometers) of Central Africa.

King Leopold II of Belgium was frustrated that, unlike the French, British, or Portuguese, tiny Belgium possessed no colonies. Yearning to rule a rich colonial empire, he persuaded Stanley to return to the Congo as his personal agent. On behalf of Leopold, Stanley signed more than 450 treaties with Congo chiefs, turning over their lands and the labor of their people to King Leopold. Clearly, the chiefs had no idea what they were signing in exchange for the cloth, trinkets, alcohol, and other cheap goods Stanley gave them. After Leopold sent agents to lobby members of Congress, the United States became the first country to recognize his claim to the Congo.

At the 1884–85 Berlin Conference, the major European powers divided Africa among themselves. King Leopold was given the Congo River Basin—an area of nearly one million square miles (2,600,000 square kilometers) and 80 times larger than Belgium. Sadly, the people of the Congo had no say in this decision. They were unaware about the conference held thousands of miles away in a distant continent and were unaware that their lives were about to tragically change.

## EUROPEAN CONTROL UNDER KING LEOPOLD

King Leopold made the newly claimed territory his own private estate and named it the Congo Free State. In an attempt to better develop its economy, he began a number of construction projects. The most ambitious was a railway that ran from the coast to Léopoldville (now Kinshasa). All of his projects were designed for a sole purpose, to facilitate the extraction and export of resources from the colony. Leopold never visited the Congo; rather, he issued decrees from Belgium. He required the natives to trade only with his agents, or with his "concessions" (private companies that paid him 50 percent of their profits).

In addition, Leopold implemented forced labor. The Congolese were required to hunt elephants for their ivory tusks and

In 1879, King Leopold II of Belgium (pictured here) hired American journalist and explorer Sir Henry Morton Stanley to establish a Belgian colony in the Congo region of Africa. The colony was formally given to Leopold and Belgium at the Berlin Conference of 1884–85, which was held to regulate European colonization and trade in Africa.

gather sap from wild rubber-producing vines growing in the rain forest. Leopold's agents held the wives and children of these male workers as hostages, often for long periods, until they returned with their quota of rubber. Following the invention of the inflatable tire, and the ensuing world rubber boom, even more workers were needed to go ever deeper into the forest in search of wild rubber. Leopold's private African army, the Force Publique (Public Force), rigorously enforced the quotas. In addition, they purchased or forcibly took slaves from Muslim slave traders to work as laborers or soldiers. (At this time, no other former or existing European colony continued the practice of slavery.)

Eventually, the Congolese began to fight back. They ambushed units of the Force Publique, fled their villages to hide in the forests, and set the rubber vine forests on fire. But Leopold's army crushed the rebellion and followed with even greater repression. They burned villages, beheaded uncooperative chiefs, and slaughtered the wives and children of men who refused to collect rubber. Force Publique soldiers were sent into the forest to find and kill hiding rebels. To prove they had succeeded, soldiers were ordered to cut off and bring back the right hand of every rebel they killed. Often, however, soldiers cut off the hands of living persons, including children, to satisfy the quota set by their officers. Needless to say, these horrible tactics succeeded in making workers collect rubber again. Leopold's profits soared, as the Congolese were brutalized.

## BREAKING KING LEOPOLD'S HOLD

Edmund Morel, a young British shipping clerk, was working in the Belgian port of Antwerp supervising the loading and unloading of ships. In the late 1890s, Morel noticed that, while the Congo Free State exported tons of raw rubber to Belgium, little was shipped back except guns and bullets. He wondered whether the many natives needed to collect the rubber were forced to do so at gunpoint.

After reading reports written by missionaries about Congo atrocities, Morel quit his shipping job and began a campaign to expose Leopold's Congo regime. As a newspaper reporter, Morel made speeches and wrote books and pamphlets condemning the mistreatment of the Congolese. To expose Leopold's bloody Congo enterprise, he used photographs and slide shows picturing children whose hands had been amputated. Morel met with U.S. President Theodore Roosevelt and enlisted the support of Booker T. Washington and Mark Twain. His activities caused the British government to investigate conditions in the Congo Free State. The report, published in 1904, uncovered widespread hostage taking, floggings, mutilation, forced labor, and murder.

Under pressure from Britain and the United States, Leopold turned over ownership of the Congo Free State to the Belgian government in 1908 in exchange for a huge cash payment. Again, the people of Congo had no say in their fate. The Belgian government eliminated the worst abuses against the native people of the Congo. But the land, along with its rubber and mineral resources, remained firmly under European control. Belgium did little to improve the well-being of the people or to involve them in administering the colony.

King Leopold's Congo Free State was an economic, environmental, cultural, and human disaster for people of the Congo. Historians estimate that 8 to 10 million people died from the violence, forced labor, and starvation caused by Leopold's lust for power and profits. When he died in 1909 at age 74, much of the world despised him. American poet Vachel Lindsay wrote this epitaph:

Listen to the yell of Leopold's ghost
Burning in Hell for his hand-maimed host,
Hear how the demons chuckle and yell
Cutting his hands off, down in Hell.

## THE NEW BELGIAN CONGO (1908–1950s)

The new era of Belgian rule in the Congo did little to change or improve conditions experienced by the Congolese. Belgium's king ruled as the head of state, through a governor-general who was responsible for daily operations. No native democratic political organizations, or even a voice in the political process, were encouraged or allowed. The Belgian administration treated the Congolese like little children who did not know what was good for them and had to be forced to do the right things. This system of colonial administration has been called *paternalistic colonialism*. Native culture and beliefs were scorned while Christian and Western values were enforced. The Roman Catholic Church emerged as the dominant religious institution, with a few Protestant denominations present. The Congolese were given curfews and other restrictions were quite common.

## RISE OF NATIONALISM

Two different nationalist movements emerged in the 1950s. One was the Mouvement National Congolais (MNC), which favored a centralized government; the other was the Association des Bakongo (ABAKO), which leaned toward a federal form of government. The MNC was the more dominant, with support in four of the six major provinces.

Led by Patrice Lumumba, a socialist-leaning and very charismatic individual, the MNC demanded immediate self-government within the framework of an African Socialism ideology. Disagreement over ideology led to a split within the MNC. Mouvement National Congolais-Kalonji, a moderate group led by Albert Kalonji, emerged. Lumumba's faction remained as Mouvement National Congolais-Lumumba. Despite philosophical differences within the party, MNC remained the most influential party in the Belgian Congo. Belgians vehemently opposed Lumumba, because they feared that their investments could be confiscated under his government.

Nevertheless, the MNC gained a clear majority in the first independent elections, and Lumumba became the first prime minister. ABAKO, led by Joseph Kasavubu, demanded immediate self-government, but preferred a federal arrangement. ABAKO control over much of the lower Congo and Léopoldville was so strong that the Belgian authorities felt threatened and banned ABAKO meetings. This led to widespread rioting in Léopoldville and the arrest of Kasavubu in 1959.

In the southern Katanga province, the situation was a little different. This region is one of tremendous mineral wealth and at the time it had the Congo's greatest European population and cultural presence. In fact, Katanga contained about 10 percent of Congo's population, but produced nearly 90 percent of the country's wealth! This fact alone provided ample incentive for self-government. Belgian settlers in Katanga and elsewhere in the country joined the nationalists in the hope of controlling the new independent nation. It soon became apparent, however, that self-government under settler rule was not a viable option. Faced with this reality, the Belgian settlers began to work closely with those African leaders who hated centralized control and desired a separate state. As a result, they supported the Confédération des Associations du Katanga (CONAKAT), which was headed by Moise Tshombe.

## ACCELERATING TOWARD INDEPENDENCE

Following widespread rioting in 1959, the Belgians hurriedly called for parliamentary elections to be held in May 1960. After a flurry of negotiations, three political alliances emerged: a coalition of federalist nationalists including ABAKO, the MNC-Lumumba, and finally a separatist alliance led by CONAKAT and Moise Tshombe. In the ensuing elections, MNC won the majority, and Patrice Lumumba became prime minister. The ABAKO coalition did so well that Kasavubu was elected president. Unfortunately, Tshombe's CONAKAT did not fare as well. They decided it was time to break away and form a new country.

On the eve of independence, the Congo was seriously underdeveloped. There were no African army officers, only three African managers in the entire civil service, and about 20 university graduates in the entire country. Although a well-established system of primary education existed, there were no institutions of higher learning. Most of the country's people were poor, poorly educated, and ill-equipped for self-government (at least on a European model). Despite the native push for independence, European investments in Congo's mineral resources were so colossal that they were determined to keep control over the country after independence.

## INDEPENDENCE AND BEYOND

On June 30, 1960, the Congo Republic declared its independence. Immediately, things began to fall apart. In the first week of July, three major events greatly impacted Congo's future. First, the army mutinied against the Belgian officers. Second, supported by Belgian settlers, Moise Tshombe declared Katanga a separate state under his leadership. Third, the many years of African suffering resulted in numerous violent attacks against Belgians. Many Belgians fled the country. In response to the crisis, without asking the Congo government, the Belgian government sent troops to protect Belgian citizens in the Congo. This was an illegal act, because the Congo was an independent nation and free from Belgian rule.

In desperation, Lumumba asked the United Nations for help. The UN sent an army of nearly 10,000 troops to restore law and order and prevent other countries from getting involved. But the UN refused to attack Katanga and Tshombe. Angry at the United Nations' refusal to act against Katanga, Lumumba asked the Soviet Union for help. The Soviets provided Lumumba's government with military equipment that gave him an opportunity to launch an attack on Katanga. This attack failed and President Kasavubu dismissed Lumumba and appointed the chief of Congo's army, Colonel Joseph Mobutu, as the new prime

Following widespread anti-European rioting in 1959, Belgian officials
came to the realization that Congo should be an independent country,
and they moved toward working with the Congolese to achieve that goal.
Pictured here are Patrice Lumumba, the leader of the Mouvement
National Congolais (MNC), and Belgian premier Gaston Eyskens during
the signing of the act of independence on June 30, 1960, in Leopoldville.

minister. Lumumba then established a rival government in Stanleyville, located in the eastern part of the country.

For the first six months of 1961, four groups claimed to
lead the Congo: 1) Mobutu's government based in Léopoldville; 2) Lumumba's group based in Stanleyville; 3) Tshombe's
"government" in Elisabethville, Katanga, and; 4) a breakaway
"government" in Kasai province led by King Albert Kalonji. The
Soviet Union supported Lumumba and Kalonji's groups. By
the summer of 1961, the country seemed to be teetering on the
brink of a vicious civil war.

## EXTERNAL INTERESTS

The rest of the world, especially the developed world, was profoundly interested in the Belgian Congo. Rich in uranium deposits, the country supplied the uranium that was used to build the American atom bombs that destroyed Hiroshima and Nagasaki, thus ending Japan's participation in World War II. The United States feared that the Soviet Union was using Lumumba to establish a Communist stronghold in Central Africa. To stop this, they planned to kill Lumumba. President Kasavubu dismissed Lumumba as prime minister and he, in turn, dismissed Kasavubu as president. Shortly after, Lumumba was arrested and assassinated. With United Nations and Soviet aid, the Katanga rebellion was brought to an end in 1963. Moise Tshombe fled the country, but was invited back by Kasavubu to be the new prime minister, as a means of easing tensions.

## A NEW ERA

Following five years of extreme instability and civil unrest, Joseph Mobutu, the Congolese army's lieutenant general, overthrew President Kasavubu in a 1965 coup d'état. A one-party political system was established, and Mobutu declared himself head of state. He ruled the country from 1965 until 1996. Relative peace and stability were achieved during his reign, although this was accomplished mostly through widespread repression of political opponents and human rights abuses. In an effort to promote the country's African heritage and spread African national awareness, Mobutu renamed the nation's cities. Léopoldville became Kinshasa, Stanleyville became Kisangani, and Elisabethville became Lumbumbashi. In 1971, he renamed the country the Republic of Zaire, and the Congo River became the Zaire River. Congolese were ordered to change their Christian names to African ones, and priests faced imprisonment if they baptized a Zairean child with a Christian name. Western attire and ties were banned. Finally, Mobutu changed his name from Joseph-Désiré Mobutu to

Mobutu Sese Seko Nkuku Ngbendu Wa Za Banga. This translates as, "The all-powerful warrior who, because of his endurance and inflexible will to win, will go from conquest to conquest, leaving fire in his wake."

Mobutu did more than win; he plundered the country's economy. Every Congolese banknote displayed his image. His portrait was exhibited in all public buildings, most businesses, and on billboards, and it was common for ordinary people to wear his likeness on their clothing. But above all, he was noted for excessive corruption. His regime gave rise to the term *kleptocracy*, or "rule by thieves." Mobutu stashed much of the country's economic output in European banks. His personal wealth included 12 French and Belgian chateaus, a Spanish castle, and a 32-bedroom Swiss villa. His personal wealth was valued at about 5 billion U.S. dollars. In his 30 years in office, he did not build a single hospital. In 1990, the average yearly income per person was a mere 170 U.S. dollars, about a tenth of what it was at independence in 1960. The once elegant city Kinshasa, the national capital, had been overrun with debris, elephant grass, and overgrown trees. It appeared as if the rain forest was claiming the capital. Mobutu left the country in terrible condition and on the brink of civil war.

## CONCLUSION

What have you learned in this chapter? The Democratic Republic of the Congo certainly has had a harsh and often violent history. Even today, conflicts that span thousands of years have yet to be resolved. Can the region ever find peace? What are the reasons for the current war and what does the future hold in regard to continuing conflict, or possible peace? These issues are addressed in the following chapter. Now it is time to explore the incredible cultural diversity of this beautiful, yet deeply divided and troubled country.

# CHAPTER

# 4

# People and Culture

The Democratic Republic of the Congo has a wonderfully rich and diverse culture (way of life). Traditional African values, beliefs, and practices have blended with those of the West to produce a distinctive and fascinating culture. In music, clothing, cuisine, and even religion, the DRC reflects the many different cultures that have influenced it throughout time. Today, thanks to such modern innovations as television, the Internet, and international travel, cultural mixing is happening at a very fast pace.

Geographers call the spread of cultural traits from place to place through time *cultural diffusion*. Diffusion can involve the spread of knowledge, values and beliefs, various practices, and material items; in fact, as you read this book and learn about the DRC, you are involved in the process of cultural diffusion! Two main types of diffusion may be identified—*expansion diffusion* and *relocation diffusion*. Let us look at an example. Do you like hip-hop music? Who is your favorite artist? Did you know that hip-hop music began in New York City among African Americans in the 1970s? Ten years later, it had spread throughout the United States, and during the 1990s, began to spread worldwide. Today, across much of the world, hip-hop music is performed in many styles and many lands, including the Democratic Republic of the Congo. Some of the most popular hip-hop artists of the Congo today include Profetzion, Fatima CIA, and the rapper Passi. You can even find some of their CDs online. Now, how did hip-hop music spread from New York City to the Congo and become Africanized? Expansion diffusion is the spread of an idea, innovation, or even a disease by contact. Starting from New York, hip-hop music gradually spread through the United States. A disease such as HIV/AIDS, which spreads mainly through sexual contact, provides another example of expansion diffusion.

Another important means of expansion diffusion is television and other media. Thanks to television, teenagers throughout the world are almost dressing the same way, wearing blue jeans and T-shirts. In the past, most cultural diffusion depended on people traveling from place to place, but in today's world of electronics, that is no longer the case. Television is everywhere. Also, travel is much faster. Thus, components of culture such as food and clothing are spreading very rapidly. In fact, you will find hamburgers, french fries, and American soft drinks served in the hotels of the Congo. Worldwide, culture seems to be converging very rapidly. Chinese food is now very much a part of American fare. Perhaps in the near future, we will find Congolese delicacies in our restaurants and grocery stores!

Relocation diffusion, on the other hand, occurs when people move and carry their culture along with them. Just as Europeans brought their languages with them, African musicians living in the United States and Belgium, for example, relocate—they go back home with the new music forms. What is most interesting is that, in cultural diffusion, the newly imported form (in this example, music) is mixed with old local

Cassava, an edible tuberous plant, is the staple crop of the Democratic Republic of the Congo. The leaves of the cassava are used like spinach or collard greens, while the root, which is pictured here, is either cooked and eaten like a potato, or dried and pounded into flour.

musical forms resulting in something completely different. You will get a good feel of this when you listen to Congolese rap music. It is hot, and different, but still hip-hop.

Food is one of the most important aspects of any culture. After all, people must eat and consume liquids in order to survive. But *what* they eat, how food is prepared, and how it is eaten is a fundamental aspect of culture. Throughout the Congo, cassava (or manioc) is the staple crop. Its fleshy tuberous root is either cooked and eaten like a potato, or dried and pounded into flour. The leaves are also used like spinach or collard greens. Cassava is easy to grow. It is high in calories, but low in protein. The most popular local beverage is palm wine. You can get palm wine ranging in taste from effervescent sweet champagne to sour wine similar to vinegar. Palm wine is made by fermenting sap, which is tapped from the male flowers of the oil palm tree (a weaker, less tasty, wine is also made from the raffia palm). A productive tree will fill an average calabash (gourd) twice a day per tapped flower. Residual yeast in the gourd rapidly ferments the juice that is ready for consumption immediately upon collection in the morning and again in the evening.

The Congo is a country of significant ethnic diversity. As many as 250 different languages can be identified within its borders. Surviving national folk traditions include pottery, the weaving of raffia, ceremonial dress and costumes, dancing styles, and music. Congolese still create masks, figurines, and stone- and nail-studded statues. Traditional masks made of rope are a specialty of the Congolese.

## SOCIAL POSITION AND STATUS

To learn about the rich culture of the Congolese people, let's go to the Mbongi, the Congolese "circle of learning." This is the place where people gather to learn how to be a part of their community. In traditional Congolese society, the problems of the community, neighbors, and families are examined and resolved at the Mbongi. On these occasions, the entire community gathers to discuss issues and pool their ideas. Mbongi involves talking, sharing, dancing, singing, chanting, and participating in rituals to mark important transitions. At the Mbongi, we will learn about your position, status, and responsibilities in society. Mostly, your age and sex determine this.

### Role of Women in Society

Ever since Belgium colonized the DRC, women have been considered to be inferior to men. In the 1930s, adult women were only considered to be legal city dwellers if they were married, widowed, or elderly. Even today, a married woman must have her husband's permission to open a bank account, accept a job, or

Many Congolese women earn money by selling goods at local markets. Appropriately known as "market women," these entrepreneurs often become quite wealthy through the sale of foodstuffs and textiles. Pictured here are Congolese women learning how to sew in hopes of selling their clothes at the local market in the southeastern town of Kalemie.

rent or sell real estate. Can you imagine what life would be like living under these restrictions? In the cities, women can work outside the home. But they are still responsible for taking care of the home, cooking, cleaning, and caring for their children. Nevertheless, women still dominate in commerce essentially as market women. They sell almost everything, including textiles, foodstuffs, fish, meat, and vegetables. Some market women are quite wealthy.

Women in rural areas have similar responsibilities, and also work on the farm to produce food to feed their family and also to sell. Because it is difficult to earn a living, farmers are often forced to sell their higher-priced and more nutritious food crops and eat whatever they can't sell. As a result, many children suffer from malnutrition.

Over the last three decades, the economy has been severely affected by internal conflict. During this period, the country's population has grown by about 3 percent each year. This combination of economic instability and rising population growth has led to a number of social and economic problems. In order to deal with these problems, families have developed several survival strategies. One such strategy is for men to move to neighboring countries in search of temporary work. Because the men are not around, the status of women has improved simply because someone has to handle the responsibilities of daily life. However, meeting family responsibilities as well as dealing with a business, or working a farm, is a high price for these women to pay.

In addition, there is always the possibility that their husbands may meet and marry another woman in the town where they are working. Polygamy is permitted. Many men return home and infect their wives with a sexually transmitted disease such as AIDS. It is a hard life for women who live in a male-dominated society.

## Role of Men

Although it seems like men lead an easy life compared to women, they also face challenges. Men traditionally are required to provide for their families with whatever is needed but is not produced in the home. They are responsible for paying for their children's education, health-care costs (there is no health insurance), clothing, transportation, and anything else that a house full of children might need. This is very difficult, because the constant state of upheaval makes regular employment nearly impossible. While men hold the highest status in society, they often bear the heaviest burden as well.

## The Elderly

The Congolese view of elderly people is much different than that of the Western world. In the DRC, elders are respected and looked up to. They are considered the wisest of all in the community and are often consulted when there is a dispute. Elders are generally not even referred to by their name by the younger generations, but are called "Elder" out of respect. If the Congolese heard of our nursing homes, they would probably not believe such places could exist! In the Congo, it is considered an honor and a duty for people to care for their elderly relatives until they die.

## Children

Congolese males often leave home at the age of 18. Females usually have to wait until they marry to leave their parents' home, but the marriage age is usually between 18 and 22. It is not very common for a person to move far away from his or her family. In Congo, your family includes not only your father, mother, and siblings, but all the extended family, including grandparents and great-grandparents. Thus, family includes all other relations, and very often they live in the same area. Another difference is how the Congolese feel toward children. Discipline is not left solely to parents. Often, the entire village is responsible for bringing up children. How would you feel if your neighbor was allowed to scold and even spank you when you did something wrong? Not a pleasant thought, is it!

## Inheritance

Throughout the Congo, inheritance and descent follow a uni-linear system instead of the dual system in the United States. That means you can inherit from your mother (matrilineal) or father (patrilineal), but not both. The extended family decides who should inherit the property of the dead person. Sometimes, fighting breaks out over who should inherit property of the deceased. Here is a typical story, which is adapted from a 2003 article from the British Broadcasting Corporation (BBC), of a family in Kinshasa squabbling over inheritance.

In early 2003, a landlord in Kinshasa named Jean-Pierre died and his poor family members fought for control of his house and the rent money it brought. The heated controversy began the day he died. While the rest of the family mourned his death, a string of uncles, brothers, and sons came to knock on the gate of the house. Each declared to the tenant that he was now the rightful owner of the house. What made the conflict worse is that all 16 people—over three generations—lived in four small rooms in the same house. Moreover, Jean-Pierre's widow accused his brothers of murdering him with witchcraft. Kinshasa's courts didn't help in the matter, either, because judges are underpaid and often corrupt. The dispute over who was the rightful owner of the house and how the rent money should have been distributed was not resolved until Jean-Pierre's wife finally decided to sell the house so that she and her children could move back to eastern Congo, where they were originally from.

## DAILY LIFE

Even the long-running war that has torn the Democratic Republic of the Congo apart cannot change the way the Congolese go about their everyday lives. Whether living in cities or rural villages, they still enjoy their music and dancing. Imagine that you were living in a farming community in the DRC. What do you think your life would be like? Well, let's see. It is four in the morning and time to wake up! You need to feed the chickens and milk the cows or goats before breakfast. Finished yet? It is time to eat and set off for school; the schoolhouse is a mile away and you have to walk! Don't forget your seat; your classroom does not have any chairs or desks. After a morning full of classes like math, grammar, and reading (in French), it is time

In the Democratic Republic of the Congo, soccer is the national sport and many children begin playing at a young age. Pictured here are two children in the town of Goma kicking a soccer ball in front of a billboard that contains the image of President Joseph Kabila.

for a break; time to play football! As in most African countries, and throughout most of the world, football (soccer) is a national pastime. All boys play and there always seems to be a match going. You run up and down the pitch (in this case, the street) chasing the ball, you turn to the right and to the left, you shoot, you score! Now it is time to go home.

As you walk down the road, you stop to watch men making bricks, the material from which all houses in your community are built. They are singing as they work. They gather mud and mix it with straw to make it stronger, and then they put the mixture into a brick press to shape it into squares. Once the bricks are shaped, they are stacked in the sun to dry. Dried bricks are then put into a brick oven to be hardened. When the fire has died and the bricks are cooled, they are sturdy and ready for use in building another home.

When you arrive at your home, it is time to start your afternoon chores. You need to feed the animals, pull weeds in the garden, and hang up the laundry to dry. Luckily, your mother already washed it by hand. By the time you finish, your mother is making fufu (a thick paste), so you help her. First, you boil plantains (like bananas) and cassava until they are soft. Then you drain off all the liquid and put the plantain and cassava mixture into a thick wooden bowl. Now the fun part begins! You take the bowl outside and hold it for your mother. She takes a long, heavy stick and pounds the mixture while you reach in and mix it with your hands. Be careful, if you don't get into a rhythm, she'll catch your hand! This process can take about an hour and continues until the fufu is smooth and thick. Once it is ready, the fufu is shaped into balls and served with soups and stews.

Now that the fufu is prepared, it is time for dinner. Your mom serves you a bowl of the delicious fufu that you helped to prepare along with okra stew. Before bed, you want to take a bath, but because your house does not have running water, you have to go out to the well and draw some. One bucket of cold water is really all you need. A quick bath, and now it is time for bed after a long day. Get a good night's rest, because morning will be here before you know it!

## ADAPTING TO ADVERSITY

The Congolese people have learned from their difficult and tumultuous past to cope with hardships. From the invasion of the Belgians, through the oppressive Mobutu regime, and the violent upheaval of Laurent Kabila's overthrow, the Congolese have had to overcome violence, bitter disappointment, and poverty. How would you cope with living in a place where it is nearly impossible to grow enough food to feed your family, and you have to sell part of what food you grow in order to buy clothes, blankets, and other essentials? Certainly, because it spends so much on war, you cannot depend upon the cash-strapped government to import enough food to feed the people. In the DRC, there are many ways of dealing with the hardships. They fall into three main categories: fight, steal, or flee.

## Fight

There are several ways in which the Congolese fight against the authority of their oppressors. One obvious way is to join the rebel armed forces, but there are other more subtle ways as well. One way is to rebel against the state's rules about what farmers are allowed to grow. Often, the government wants farmers to grow "cash crops" such as coffee and tobacco, rather than raising food crops to feed their family. Would you want to work all day harvesting coffee for the government to sell over-seas and then go home to no food? Well, the Congolese people don't want to, either! So they often ignore the government's edict and grow what they need. Workers' unions are another way to fight an unfair system. Although under Mobutu's reign workers' unions were crushed at the first sign of resistance, they have begun to emerge again in the cities, where there are large factories.

## Steal

Unfortunately, the rampant corruption in the government, which has existed since the founding of the Belgian colony, has produced a culture of corruption among citizens as well. Asking for bribes is considered an everyday practice in the DRC, as it is throughout much of Africa. In fact, it would be considered strange if officials did not ask for "dash" (as bribes are called). Teachers are bribed for good grades, doctors are bribed for medicine, judges are bribed for verdicts, government officials are bribed for licenses, and banks are bribed for loans. The list goes on and on. Can you imagine having to pay a bribe in order to get almost any service? Would you want to start a business in a country where bribes had to be paid at every turn in order to become established?

## Flee

Those who can afford to will often flee the country, or at least send their families overseas to safety. People who are unable to flee oversees may simply go to a neighboring country (there are nine to choose from, can you remember them?). Flight is becoming a much more common way to avoid the continuing conflict. In fact, there are refugee camps set up all along the DRC's borders for those who make it out of the country. Many countries throughout the world have accepted Congolese refugees. South Africa, England, and the United States have the highest percentage of these escapees, many of whom apply for political asylum. Have you ever met a person who fled the Congo? If so, you can now talk intelligently with them about the problems their country faces and better understand why they left!

## RELIGION

Religion is considered by some to be another coping method employed by the Congolese. In fact, religion is an important part of daily life in the DRC. People go to church to feel a sense of community and to find support. Nearly everyone belongs to a church of some kind. Christianity is by far the most prevalent religion. About 50 percent of the population profess Roman Catholicism, 20 percent embrace Protestantism, and 10 percent belong to the Kimbanguist Church, which is the Congolese version of European Christianity. Only about 10 percent of the population is Muslim, adherents of the Islamic faith. The last

For many Congolese, religion has become a coping method to deal with the numerous difficulties they face. Approximately 70 percent of Congolese are Christians, including this family who is attending a church service in the town of Bunia, in the northeastern part of the country.

10 percent embrace traditional Congolese beliefs. These are the beliefs that come to mind when we think about African religion: witch doctors, divination, and possession by spirits. Witches are considered evil and in most cases are thrown out of their homes and shunned by their communities, even if they are children. Many of the street children who roam the Congo's cities have met this fate. Known as "witch children," they are often forced to live in cemeteries and only come out at night. And they often end up following the very occult practices for which they were shunned by society.

## FUN TIME

So, what do the Congolese do for fun? Well, we already know about football, but what else is there for them to do? The

Congolese love music, especially Rumba and Soukous, which is their own Rumba variation. Soukous became popular in the 1930s and spread throughout Africa. Today, it is known throughout Europe and its popularity continues to spread. Dance clubs are very popular in the cities, and in the rural areas people love to get together to play music and dance. Even when life is difficult, there is much to celebrate, and the Congolese are good at celebrating! Even their clothing is fun! Bright, bold colors are used to make clothing for men and women, although men tend to wear more Westernized clothing than do most women. Traditional dresses and head wraps in beautiful greens, blues, pinks, reds, and many other colors can be seen wherever you look! In a nation where little else is within their control, the people place a heavy emphasis on looking their best and taking pride in their appearance. Before we leave the Congo, let's pay a quick visit to the Pygmies, the indigenous people of the country.

## PYGMIES OF THE CONGO

Pygmies are the earliest known inhabitants of the Congo forests. The best-known tribe, the Mbuti, or Bambuti, average 51 inches (130 centimeters) in height and are the shortest of all human groups. They live mostly in the Ituri forest in northeastern Congo. Despite their diminutive stature, Pygmies are skilled hunters. Historically a migratory people, today they tend to be less mobile, living in one location and residing in round or rectangular one-family huts made of branches and leaves called *mongulus*. These shelters are normally built by women.

The Mbuti live in small bands of fewer than 50 members. Each band has its own territory, but if the food supply runs out, they will move to a different territory. Inter-band marriages are common, and individuals are free to leave one band and join another. Marriage is by sister exchange. A man must arrange the marriage of one of the female members of his band to a man in his prospective bride's band. Normally monogamous,

Pygmies have a strong family structure. A band has no formal leaders; rather, problems are solved through open discussions.

## CONCLUSION

So, what have you learned about the Congolese culture; the way these people live and what they do? The Congolese are hard-working and industrious. They make most of what they use, and take care of what they have. They are a loving and warm-hearted people, who embrace neighbors and strangers alike. Their idea of family encompasses even their distant relatives, and they respect and care for their elders. Even though the Congolese have hard lives, they know how to have fun, and they love to celebrate. They consider religion part of their daily lives, and it is extremely important to them. They love music and dancing, especially hip-hop in the urban areas. In a world that is rapidly changing, they have managed to preserve their culture, and through it, their history, incorporating the old ways with the new. They have adapted, and will survive.

# 5

# Government
# and Economy

In most nations, government and economy go hand in hand. That
is, if government is stable, so, too, will the country's economy
thrive. If, on the other hand, the government fails at its job of
maintaining stability, the economy will suffer. Because of this close
link, in this chapter government and economy are presented together.
From the day King Leopold II established colonial authority until
today, government in the Congo has always been unstable. This is
reflected in the country's seven name changes since 1885: Congo Free
State (1885–1908), Belgian Congo (1908–1960), Republic of the
Congo-Léopoldville (1960–1964), Democratic Republic of the
Congo-Léopoldville (1964–1966), Democratic Republic of the
Congo-Kinshasa (1966–1971), Republic of Zaire (1971–1997), and
finally Democratic Republic of the Congo (since 1997).

The Congo has vast natural resources and mineral wealth, but
remains one of the world's poorest countries. An excellent potential

exists for development of a tourist-based economy, but it remains largely undeveloped. Tourists are not attracted to locations where little if any infrastructure (hotels, restaurants, roads and vehicles, etc.) exists or where their lives might be in jeopardy. The vast hydroelectric potential of the Congo River remains untapped. Congo has vast mineral resources. There are rich deposits of gold, silver, and diamonds; industrial metals include cobalt, copper, zinc, manganese, and tin; deposits of petroleum, uranium, and coal give the country sources of energy. Instead of developing these potentials, however, the Congo merely exports agricultural products and raw materials. Main cash crops include coffee, palm oil, rubber, cotton, sugar, tea, and cocoa. Food crops include cassava, plantains, maize, groundnuts, and rice. In order to develop, a country must have adequate transportation and communication linkages, power and communication networks, and sanitation and other essential facilities. In the DRC, most of these essential elements are sparse or even absent altogether. All of these problems can be traced to three primary factors. First, since the beginning, the country has been very poorly governed; second, this potentially rich land has been torn and impoverished by war; finally, the DRC, as is true throughout much of Africa, is making the difficult transition from a traditional "folk" (self-sufficient) economy to a modern economy based on industry and commerce.

Of all currently existing possibilities for economic development, few if any offer greater potential than does tourism. This beautiful "Amazon Basin of Africa" is covered with endless rain forest, rugged mountains and volcanoes, the world's greatest rift valley, enormous rivers, and abundant wildlife. Its several national parks provide a showcase for mountain gorillas, lowland gorillas, chimpanzees, and many other forms of animal life. Some of the great lakes of East Africa—Tanganyika, Kivu, Edward, and Albert—are located at the Congo's eastern border. Le Grand Pousseur, the Congo riverboat between Kinshasa and Kisangani, offers one of Africa's classic journeys. The vessel is essentially a floating village that can accommodate up to 2,000 people. Unfortunately, the dark cloud of war stands in the way of further developing these possible tourist attractions.

The huge potential of the Congo River is underutilized. With a length of 2,720 miles (4,375 kilometers), it is Africa's second-longest river (the Nile is the world's longest). At its widest point, the river spans a width of about 10 miles (16 kilometers). The Congo contains some 4,000 islands, some as long as 10 miles (16 kilometers). Upstream from Livingstone Falls, over which the river cascades about 100 miles (160 kilometers) from its mouth, the Congo is navigable for long distances. And the mighty stream has tremendous potential for hydroelectric power generation. In the absence of railroads or adequate highways, the river is the main access artery into the country's interior. This is because most roads are unpaved and in need of repair. Most people rely on waterways and the usually overcrowded ferries and barges that travel along them. Deadly accidents are quite frequent on the Congo. In November 2005, more than 200 people died when a ferry sank during a storm.

In many ways, Congo is less well off today than it was a half-century ago. Few Congolese have access to roads, electricity, clean water, medical care, or almost any other public services. The formal (cash) economy has virtually collapsed. In 2005, the average per-capita income was 120 U.S. dollars, one of the world's lowest rates. Life expectancy is about 50 years for men and 53 years for women (about 20 years lower than the average for the world's less developed countries). Central Bank estimates showed inflation running at a staggering 520 percent in 2000, although this figure has been greatly reduced. The country ranks near the very bottom of the Human Development Index, an indicator of human well-being. How did this happen in a country with so much potential?

Due to a lack of adequate highways, Congolese often turn to ferries to transport them from place to place. Unfortunately, ferries, such as the one pictured here, are often overcrowded, and deadly accidents frequently occur on the country's waterways.

## THE MOBUTU SESE SEKO REGIME (1965–1997)

Early in his rule, Mobutu consolidated power by publicly executing political rivals, secessionists, coup plotters, and other threats to his rule. Initially, he nationalized foreign-owned firms and forced European investors, managers, and technicians out of the country. In many cases, he handed the management of these firms to relatives and close associates who not only were inept, but often stole assets. The absence of well-trained and experienced Europeans caused such an economic slump that, by 1977, Mobutu was forced to try to convince them to come back. In the same year, he desperately needed Belgian assistance to repulse an attack on Katanga by rebels based in Angola. Despite the many problems that could directly be attributed to Mobutu's inept leadership, he was reelected in 1977. Of course his victory was assisted by the fact that no other candidates were allowed to challenge him in the election!

Mobutu worked hard to increase his personal fortune at the expense of his country and its people. In fact, by 1984, it was estimated that he was worth nearly 5 billion U.S. dollars, most of which was safely stashed away in Swiss banks. This figure was about the same amount as the country's foreign debt at the time. In 1989, the government defaulted on international loans from Belgium. Amazingly, the Congo was the world's fourth-largest producer of industrial diamonds during the 1980s. Yet because of widespread corruption and the diversion of public resources for personal gain, the country's economy continued to decline. In the early 1990s, the unrecorded and illicit trans-actions of Zaire's unofficial economy were estimated to be three times greater than the country's official gross domestic product (the value of all goods and services produced).

Mobutu owned a fleet of luxury vehicles that he used to travel between his numerous palaces, while many of his people starved. The country's infrastructure virtually collapsed, and many public workers went months without being paid. Only members of the Special Presidential Division, Mobutu's body-guards, were adequately paid on a regular basis. Mobutu's rule earned a reputation as one of the world's foremost examples of *kleptocracy* (rule by theives) and *nepotism* (favoring relatives or personal friends).

Despite Mobutu's blatant mismanagement and brutality, he continued to receive loans and assistance from the United States, other Western countries, and international organiza-tions such as the International Monetary Fund. Most Western nations supported his regime because of his pro-Western, anti-Communist stance. Their policy was "Mobutu or chaos." Trans-lated, this meant that without Mobutu, Zaire would become politically unstable and prone to civil war, ethnic violence, or something worse. Zaire's strategic location in the center of the continent and vast mineral wealth were further reasons for the support of Mobutu by Western nations.

Budgetary imbalance, inflation, and debt consistently plagued the Mobutu government despite World Bank and International Monetary Fund (IMF) assistance. In early 1990, both the World Bank and the IMF suspended aid to Zaire. Due to the rising economic crisis, Mobutu agreed to allow the formation of other political parties, appointed a transitional government, and promised to hold elections. Following riots in Kinshasa by unpaid soldiers, he brought members of opposition parties into a coalition government, but continued to control the security services and important ministries.

Political divisions led to the creation of two governments in 1993; one for and one against Mobutu. Without World Bank and IMF support, the economic situation became extremely critical. For most people, life was very difficult. A new currency, the New Zaire (NZ), was introduced to try to curb inflation. Despite the new currency, inflation rose to more than 9,000 percent by early 1994. That year, the two governments joined together to form the High Council of Republic Parliament of Transition (HCR-PT). Yet that did not solve the problem. For the next two years, Mobutu aggressively struggled to maintain power, but his government was rapidly falling apart.

During the Rwandan genocide of 1994, Mobutu had openly supported Hutu extremists who murdered hundreds of thousands of Tutsis in that country and forced thousands more to seek exile in Zaire. When Mobutu's government issued an order in November 1996 that forced Tutsis to leave the country on penalty of death, they erupted in rebellion. From eastern Zaire, with the support of Rwandan president Paul Kagame, they launched an attack to overthrow Mobutu, joining forces with Congolese who opposed Mobutu as they marched west toward Kinshasa. This was the beginning of the First Congo War. Mobutu's underpaid and ill-equipped army crumbled in

Joseph Mobutu, who is pictured here with then-President George H. W. Bush in 1989, took control of Congo in 1965, after he overthrew President Joseph Kasavubu in a coup d'état. Mobutu ruled the country until 1997 and set about a course to promote African heritage by instituting several reforms, including changing the names of the country's cities, banning Western attire, and ordering citizens to adopt African names.

front of the march, and Mobutu was overthrown on May 16, 1997. Led by Laurent-Désiré Kabila, the Tutsi rebels and other anti-Mobutu groups captured Kinshasa. Kabila became the new president and renamed the country Democratic Republic of the Congo.

## Gbadolite, Congo's Most Curious Town

When Mobutu was president of the Congo, Gbadolite, a small town deep in the vast forests of northern Congo, was a very special place. It had wide boulevards, grand brick houses, and an international airport. The population, many of whom were relatives of Mobutu, had electricity and plumbing. They also held jobs, working as servants in the three palaces that Mobutu had built around the town.

Disaster struck in 1997, when Mobutu was removed from power. Led by Laurent Kabila, Congolese rebels passed through the town and in a frenzy, they attacked the palaces, stole hundreds of luxury cars, and stripped the town of anything and everything of value that they could carry away. Today, Gbadolite is a shadow of its old self. The fabled palaces have been vandalized and the walls are covered with graffiti. The four-story state lodge has been stripped bare, leaving only black sunken bathtubs and monstrous chandeliers, too heavy for looters to cart away. Mobutu's pet leopard is said to stalk the overgrown gardens. How times change! For 30 years, Gbadolite was the favored hometown of an extravagant dictator. Now the people desperately crave a normal life, one with jobs—any jobs.

## THE LAURENT KABILA REGIME (1997–2001)

In 1997, Laurent Kabila created the Public Salvation Government. His government was dominated by the Alliance of Democratic Forces for the Liberation of Congo-Zaire (ADFL), a coalition of Congolese dissidents, disgruntled minority groups, and nations that toppled President Mobutu. Prominent among these governments were Rwanda and Uganda. The Kabila government began a program of economic reconstruction, and he focused initially on the corrupt tax system, the civilian police force, and repairing the road system. He was successful at improving internal security and lowering the inflation rate in his first year as president. However, Kabila ruled like a dictator. All executive, legislative, and military powers were vested in him. Although the legal system was supposed to be independent, he dismissed and appointed judges at will. Despite claims that his was a transitional government leading to a new constitution and full elections by April 1999, these elections were not held. Soon, the ADFL fell apart.

Despite some successes, Kabila was unable to control insurgent activities by various armed groups. The Hutu *Interahamwe* ("Those Who Stand Together," or "Those Who Fight Together") worked to destabilize the Kabila regime; so did Mai-Mai soldiers (a variety of Congolese militia groups formed to resist the invasion of Rwandese forces) and a February 1998 mutiny by Tutsi *Banyamulenge* (a group of Tutsis living in the eastern region of the Congo). In addition, Kabila's pledges to democratize the government over time were proved to be false when he banned political parties and increasingly centralized power. Criticism of Kabila's government grew both within the country and within the international community.

In an attempt to stabilize the country and consolidate his control, in August 1998, President Kabila expelled the Rwandan troops remaining in the DRC. This prompted army mutinies in Kinshasa and the Kivu provinces in the east. Although the Kinshasa mutiny was put down, the mutiny in the Kivus continued and mushroomed into a drive to topple the government. Thus began the Second Congo War. Opposing the Kabila government were the armies of Rwanda and Uganda, and factions of the Rally for Congolese Democracy (RCD). The Movement for the Liberation of Congo (MLC), another rebel group, emerged later. Defending the Kabila government were Angola, Namibia, Chad, Zimbabwe, and the Congolese Army.

At the time war broke out in the DRC in August 1998, some progress had been made in the economic reconstruction of the country. But major problems continued to exist in transportation infrastructure, customs administration, and the tax system. Government finances had not been put in order, and relations with the IMF and World Bank were in disarray. The outbreak of war caused a major decline in economic activity that continues to the present. A cease-fire was signed on July 10, 1999, but sporadic fighting continued. Kabila was assassinated on January 16, 2001, and his son Joseph Kabila was named head of state 10 days later.

After becoming president of the Democratic Republic of the Congo in January 2001, Joseph Kabila's main concern was removing foreign troops from the country and bringing the civil war to an end. In July 2002, Kabila and Rwandan president Paul Kagame agreed to a peace accord, and three months later, Rwandan troops pulled out of eastern Congo.

## THE JOSEPH KABILA REGIME (2001–PRESENT)

Upon becoming president, Joseph Kabila's first priority was negotiating peace. He received considerable assistance from the United Nations and many Western industrialized countries. The African Union and the UN both sent peacekeepers. In October 2002, Joseph Kabila was successful in getting Rwandan forces to withdraw from eastern Congo. Two months later, an agreement was signed by all remaining warring parties to end the fighting and set up a government of national unity.

Following the 2002 peace agreement, an interim administration was set up in 2003. Joseph Kabila remains president, with four vice presidents representing the former government, former rebel groups, and the political opposition. Yet, the instability continues. On March 28, 2004, a coup attempt around the capital of Kinshasa, allegedly organized by supporters of the late president Mobutu Sese Seko, failed. On June 11, 2004, coup plotters led by Major Eric Lenge declared that the country's peace process was not working and attempted to take power; however, the attempt was thwarted by loyalist troops.

Despite efforts to end the fighting, Kabila's government has almost no military control over the chaotic eastern regions, particularly the Ituri district. The revamped Congolese Army is a combination of Kabila's allies and former rebel militias. In July 2005, a hundred members of one of these militias went on a rampage in a major town near Kinshasa, killing a number of civilians. Congo's civil war, in which an estimated 3.9 million people have died since 1996, has been called the bloodiest war in history because of the extreme brutality with which it is associated. Sadly, it continues.

## TODAY'S GOVERNMENT

In December 2005, the Congolese people were finally able to vote to ratify a new constitution, which set the stage for the 2006 elections. On July 30, 2006, the DRC held its first multiparty elections since the country gained independence in 1960. Joseph Kabila captured 45 percent of the vote, while Jean-Pierre Bemba of the Movement for the Liberation of the Congo (MLC) captured 20 percent. The voting process, though technically difficult due to the lack of infrastructure, was organized and conducted by the Congolese Independent Electoral Commission with support from the United Nations. Many Congolese have complained that the constitution is so ambiguous in its wording that they are unsure what it actually says. Part of the problem, of course, is the country's very low rate of literacy; only about two-thirds of the population can read at even a very elementary level. However, President Kabila urged the Congolese people to vote "Yes," insisting that the new constitution is the country's best hope for peace in the future.

Twenty-five million Congolese turned out for the two-day balloting and approved the constitution. Hopefully, the government will soon be undergoing positive changes. IMF and World Bank missions have met with the new government to develop a coherent economic plan. The future, however, remains quite uncertain. In fact, the DRC appears to be barely holding on, supported by the UN peacekeeping forces and international aid. How long this can be sustained remains to be seen. The eastern part of the country remains particularly volatile. Rwanda and Uganda may one day fully take control of the DRC. In 2005, the International Court of Justice ruled that Uganda must compensate the Democratic Republic of the Congo for rights abuses and the plundering of resources between 1998 and 2003.

To summarize, war and political instability have ruined the DRC's economy. The war has dramatically reduced government revenue and greatly increased external debt. Foreign businesses have cut operations due to uncertainty associated with the conflict and increased government harassment and restrictions. The huge difference between the official and the black market rate for foreign currency led to widespread use of U.S. dollars for domestic commercial transactions. Poor infrastructure, an uncertain legal framework, corruption, and lack of openness in government economic policy and financial operations remain a major obstacle to foreign investment. The DRC experienced negative economic growth in 2000, but conditions improved in late 2002 with the withdrawal of a large portion of the invading foreign troops. It appears that Congo's economy needs only one remedy—an end to the war! But will it ever come?

A mid-August 2006 Reuters news release headline read: "Gunfights as Congo heads for presidential run-off." The following article begins, "Congolese President Joseph Kabila's

guards fought gun battles with forces loyal to election chal-
lenger Jean-Pierre Bemba in the capital Kinshasa." This unrest
in the streets of Kinshasa led to 16 deaths and a call for a second round of elections to be held at the end of October 2006.
In the Democratic Republic of the Congo, it seems that the
more things change, the more they stay the same.

# CHAPTER

# 6

# Living in the Congo Today

How would you like to live in a place where you were afraid to walk down the street because you might be shot? What if you could not sleep at night because a group of armed rebels might break into your house and kill you and your entire family? What if you could not even trust the police to protect you because they might do the same things as the militias? These are exactly the fears of young people in the DRC. Think of the very worst place in your country. Perhaps some inner-city ghetto comes to mind—a place where grinding poverty, warring gangs, and rampant drug dealing contribute to frequent violence. Now, imagine that the entire country was like that! It still does not compare to the reality facing Congolese citizens. In the DRC, young and old alike are not even safe from their own people. In the past, rebel groups tortured and killed people because of their different ethnic backgrounds. Today, they are just as apt to kill their own people in order to steal their clothes, jewelry, or other possessions. This is the harsh reality facing your generation and all others in the DRC.

The Democratic Republic of the Congo is one of the world's poorest countries. A third of all children are born underweight and about two of every five youngsters under five years of age are stunted by malnutrition. Out of every 1,000 children born, about 95 die before their first birthday, contributing to one of the world's highest infant mortality rates. (By comparison, the figures for the United States and Canada are 5.2 and 4.8, respectively.) The Congo's sad condition is the result of many factors, including, but by no means limited to, years of warfare. Let us look at what life is like today.

## THE GEOGRAPHY OF CONFLICT

Life in the Democratic Republic of the Congo is very difficult. Warring factions have destroyed many of the schools. Even where schools exist, because of widespread poverty, education is not a priority for many parents or local authorities. Lack of basic health and social services compound the problem. The eastern part of the country bordering Rwanda and Uganda, in particular, is worse off than elsewhere in this troubled land.

The Ituri provinces and South Kivu, in the eastern part of the country, have experienced some of the worst violence. In this area, many thousands have died in the last five years due to ethnic violence between Hemas and Lendus. In September 2002, about 1,200 Hema civilians were killed in the village of Nyakunde. In May 2003, after a seven-month Hema rule that left 10,000 Lendus dead, the Lendus launched an attack, massacring Lendu and Hema civilians by the thousands and causing 250,000 to flee. The Hema militia used weapons supplied by nearby Uganda. When the fighting subsided, child soldiers began looting the town, stealing clothes, food, and jewelry. The fighting in this one province claimed more than 50,000 lives between the years 2000 and 2003. For a while, the area replaced

Sudan's Darfur region as being the world's worst humanitarian crisis. Fighting continues to kill thousands of people every month. Militias kidnap, torture, and murder civilians, or force them to work as fishermen, servants, or sex slaves. The UN has even reported cannibalism in the region.

## POVERTY AND DISEASE—CONSEQUENCES OF WAR

Certainly not every part of the nation is so horribly affected by the war as the Ituri and South Kivu provinces, but every area is affected in some way. Poverty and all of its consequences ravage the entire country and affect all of its citizens. Among the worst effects of poverty is the rise in prostitution. Men, women, and children are selling their bodies because they have nothing else to sell. They have no other way to make enough money to provide the most basic necessities of life, such as food, clothing, and shelter. Girls as young as 9 and 10 are having sex with much older men, especially the military, for less than one dollar. These are the terrible choices that face so many Congolese people every day.

Unfortunately, that is not the worst of the situation. Sexual violence by militias, the national army, and even outside United Nations peacekeepers against civilians is widespread. As a result, the rate of sexually transmitted disease is feared to be very high. The rapid spread of HIV/AIDS is a particular source of concern. This is the type of problem that medical geographers study.

Medical geographers are concerned with where diseases occur, and why they occur in their area of distribution, and their effect on society. By mapping the distribution of diseases, a medical geographer can determine where they occur. He or she can then begin to search for causal relationships that may explain the patterns of distribution. The idea is that if we can understand what drives the spread of disease, we have a better chance of slowing its transmission. In the DRC, for example, there is a correlation between areas of political instability and higher rates of sexually transmitted infections. It is known that in these areas, rape is used as a political weapon. With many soldiers and refugees coming from Uganda and Rwanda, countries with high HIV/AIDS rates, it is assumed that many Congolese have been infected. Yet, due to the war, getting accurate data on HIV/AIDS and other diseases is extremely difficult. To make matters worse, because of the ongoing instability within the region, there is little opportunity for testing or treating the disease.

HIV is not the only health concern in the DRC. Periodic outbreaks of Ebola hemorrhagic fever are common. No cure exists for this viral infection that also kills chimpanzees. In the 1970s, severe outbreaks in Sudan and the DRC killed approximately 440 people. The strain of the virus in the DRC is extremely deadly, killing about 90 percent of its victims. Usually, flu-like symptoms such as a sore throat, headache, and high temperature are the first signs of infection. Nausea, vomiting, and diarrhea follow. Ebola causes high fever, diarrhea, and bleeding from the nose and gums, as well as massive internal bleeding. Bodily discharges, including urine, are laden with the virus. In fact, if you touch the corpse of an animal or person who died from Ebola, you can catch the virus. That makes burying the dead very dangerous. In addition, pneumonic plague is also a problem. In 2005, at least 60 people died from the disease in the country's northeastern section. The plague affects the lungs and is fatal if left untreated. Those who died were mostly diamond miners. To avoid the disease, many people simply fled. Unfortunately, as people flee to avoid disease, they carry the disease to new locations.

Finally, diseases previously regarded as being eradicated, such as polio, bubonic plague, and whooping cough, have resurfaced again due to lack of access to health care. Tuberculosis has increased, and outbreaks of measles, cholera, and meningitis also have been reported. In addition to all these, malaria persists as the leading cause of illness. It accounts for

Approximately 30,000 of the Democratic Republic of the Congo's children are soldiers. The young boys pictured here are members of a Ugandan-supported Congolese rebel movement in the northeastern DRC town of Bunia.

about 90 percent of all hospital visits and about one-half of all deaths, especially among children under five.

## CHILD SOLDIERS

Do you ever think to yourself, "I have such a hard life"? If so, you are like most teenagers. The next time you hold this thought, however, remember that in many parts of the world people literally kill to have a fraction of what people living in the developed world consider "the basics." Adequate food, shelter, and clothing certainly are never guaranteed to most Congolese citizens. Neither is the freedom to say what you want, to think how you want, or to go where you want to live!

Not even the freedom to live is guaranteed to children in the DRC. About 30,000 of the country's children are soldiers, either with the national army or some rebel group. Some are kidnapped and forced to join the military. Others join because they are promised food, clothes, and money. All of them are forced to kill. Emmanuele and Serge are two such soldiers. Emmanuele joined a rebel group at the age of 15 because he had no money. The group forced him to fight on the front lines and they beat him if he refused to fight. Serge was taken from his school at the age of eight. He was taken to Bunia and forced to work on a roadblock and ordered to kill anyone who tried to pass without permission.

Many of the DRC's child soldiers are girls. Vumilla, Furaa, and Hawa are three of these. At the age of 11, Furaa was seized by a rebel group, forced to fight on the front lines, and given to one of the rebels to be his wife. At the age of 13, she and her newborn daughter were rescued and taken to a UNICEF camp. Vumilla was orphaned by the war. She was given the standard $15, food, and a uniform, and in return, she gave up her childhood to fight and kill. Hawa was 13 when three soldiers raped her outside her home. It was another five months before she realized she was pregnant. Now, at 15, with a small child, life is very difficult.

Groups such as UNICEF and Save the Children have set up camps in order to care for these children and hopefully reintegrate them back into their communities. For some, this is impossible, as families and entire communities have been destroyed. In other cases, communities are unwilling to take back the children. They are resentful that in some cases the youngsters carried out atrocities, killing friends and neighbors when ordered to do so. Sadly, that is the case with Serge. After waiting for months to be reunited with his family, he learned that his father did not want him back. With no place to go, Serge and others like him become street children. It is extremely sad that children who were forced from their homes and into a war would become outcasts because of circumstances beyond their control. It is also dangerous. Children who have been trained to use violence from such a young age are far more likely to kill in order to get what they want.

## ARE CONGO'S NEIGHBORS ENEMIES OR FRIENDS?

The eastern part of the Democratic Republic of the Congo is critically unstable, because it is rich in minerals that others want to control. It also borders troubled Uganda, Rwanda, and Burundi. All of these countries have their own internal conflicts that have spilled over into the Congo. And all of them have intervened militarily in the DRC. Rwanda and Uganda are the two most important.

Rwanda is a tiny, poor, mountainous state that is heavily overpopulated, has few natural resources, and only moderately productive soil. But, it has one of the most powerful armies in the region. Recently, it went through a devastating civil war that led to the massacre of about a million people. This conflict resulted in one of the worst cases of ethnic cleansing in history. The 2004 movie *Hotel Rwanda*, directed by Terry George, tells the story of this massacre. Rwanda's conflict was between the Hutu and the Tutsi tribes. The Hutu are traditional farmers, and the Tutsi are nomadic goatherders. The Tutsi comprise only 14 percent of Rwanda's population. Yet, like feudal lords, they dominated the Hutu (about 85 percent of the population) and the much smaller Twa Pigmy minority. During the colonial era, the Belgians used the Tutsi minority as puppets to rule the country for many years. In the outbreak of violence, Hutu and Tutsi militias attacked each other resulting in more than one million deaths in about 100 days of heated fighting.

Rwanda has twice invaded the eastern region of the Democratic Republic of the Congo. The neighboring country covets the DRC's gold, tin ore, rare gems, and other minerals. Once, it attempted to topple the Mobutu regime and on a second occasion it tried to flush out remnants of the ethnic Hutu army that committed the Rwandan genocide of 1994. Rwanda argues that the Interahamwe, or armed Hutus, who are hiding in the forests of Congo, are a threat to civilian Tutsis in Rwanda. Yet, as Congo descended into chaos, Rwanda immediately began to prosper. Suddenly, the country was exporting up to $20 million (in U.S. dollars) worth of coltan (a rare metallic ore used in electronic devices such as cell phones) each month. And diamond exports miraculously jumped from 166 carats in 1998 to 30,500 in 2000! Neither mineral is prevalent in Rwanda.

Uganda makes millions of dollars each week by pillaging gold, diamonds, and other minerals from the DRC. These riches are shipped to Uganda from the mines in the parts of eastern Congo controlled by the Ugandan Army. The gold is then bought by private companies and exported once more, this time from Uganda, thereby improving that country's balance of trade. Uganda does not produce gold, but thanks to the war in Congo, gold has become the second-largest export earner after coffee, bringing in more than 100 million U.S. dollars a year, according to the latest government statistics. In 2005, the International Court of Justice ordered Uganda to pay 10 billion U.S. dollars to the DRC as compensation for the invasion.

Globally, the price of metals is at a 10-year high and rising. This factor has intensified the fierce competition for the storehouse of riches in eastern DRC. New environmental regulations in Japan and Western Europe, forcing manufacturers to use tin instead of lead in printed circuit boards, are a major factor driving up demand and prices. According to the United Nations, control over mineral resources has always been a significant factor in the DRC war. The commercial interest the outside world has in Congolese gold, timber, diamonds, and other minerals drew six neighboring states into the DRC's many-sided war from 1998 to 2003.

## STRUGGLE FOR STABILITY

In the late 2004 and 2005, the world was shocked and saddened by several huge natural disasters. In Southeast Asia, a giant tsunami killed an estimated 250,000 people; a huge earthquake struck northern Pakistan and killed thousands more; in the southern United States, Hurricane Katrina was responsible for more than 1,000 deaths, hundreds of thousands of people being displaced, and billions of dollars in property damage. These are the stories that attracted widespread media attention and that people will remember. Yet, in the Democratic Republic of the Congo, it is estimated that more than 30,000 people are killed *each* month and nearly 3 million people have had to flee their homes during recent years. That means that in a single year, three times as many people died in the DRC as a result of violence than lost their lives in the three aforementioned natural disasters combined. Adding to the widespread grief that is commonplace among Congolese, they also have had to cope with a natural disaster of their own. In December 2005, an earthquake caused by tectonic activity in the Great Rift Valley occurred beneath Lake Tanganyika. The tremor killed or injured hundreds of people, most of whom were trapped by and buried beneath collapsing houses.

How do you suppose the Congolese are able to keep going about their daily lives with so much tragedy all around them? Certainly, through time, they have developed a very strong will to survive in the face of numerous conflicts that confront them on an almost daily basis. In fact, many Congolese believe that life is actually getting better. They have just passed a new constitution and in 2006 were in the process of electing a new president. The national railway, closed by fighting for six years, was reopened in 2005. The train often derails, and a 560-mile (900-kilometer) journey generally takes two weeks to complete. Nonetheless, citizens are excited, because they finally have a way to travel across the country.

## TODAY'S OUTLOOK

Although the Congolese are constantly faced with more hardship than we can imagine, they continue to go on with their lives. When armed groups raze their villages, the survivors bury the victims, rebuild their homes, and harvest what is left of their crops. The constant bloodshed has become an accepted

On July 30, 2006, the Democratic Republic of the Congo held its first multiparty elections since the country gained independence in 1960. President Joseph Kabila, the incumbent, won 45 percent of the popular vote, but a runoff election had to be held, because neither Kabila or his opponent, Jean-Pierre Bemba, won a majority of votes.

part of life for these men, women, and children. Although some are civilians and others are soldiers, all are the victims of a corrupt rule that they have been unable to escape. We can understand why it is so important to these people to be given the opportunity to vote. Through the democratic process, they believe that they can make a difference in their country's future, hence, their own. Many are optimistic that they can get their country back on track and move forward toward a more peaceful future.

# 7

# The Democratic Republic of the Congo Looks Ahead

The story of the Congo is disturbingly sad. After 75 years of harsh colonial rule marked by the plundering of resources and other wealth and the rape and murder of citizens, the Belgians left very abruptly. Fueled by external interests, these widespread atrocities continued after independence, particularly under President Mobutu. In February 2006, a new constitution was introduced and with it was unfurled a new national flag. The world's biggest peacekeeping force, with some 17,000 troops and police, is trying to restore order and control lawless militia fighters. But the United Nations peacekeeping force struggles for lack of strong leadership and a shocking lack of discipline among its troops. The national army, forged from various rival armed factions, remains disunited and largely ineffective.

Today, the rape and plunder of the Congo's people and natural resources continues. It is not at all uncommon for women to be raped in front of their family, in the presence of their shocked and helpless children and husband. Rape as a weapon of war is nothing new; what is unusual in the DRC is its widespread occurrence and the relative indifference of the outside world.

The DRC's beautiful forests and valuable stores of minerals also are under siege. In rain forests, logging companies are cutting their way to huge profits leaving huge tracts of wasteland behind. Tax revenues derived from wealth gained by the pillaging of forest resources remain very low. Although anyone who cuts a tree is required by law to replant one or two trees, companies and individuals largely ignore this ruling. In this chaotic environment, laws are rarely enforced. Most timber is exported as logs, rather than processed wood, thereby exporting much-needed jobs as well. Considering the many problems it faces, one can simply wonder how long the Democratic Republic of the Congo will be able to survive.

## ELECTIONS OR BUST

As mentioned previously, President Joseph Kabila set a late July 2006 date of the first multiparty democratic election in the DRC's 46-year history as an independent nation. Millions of voters enthusiastically flocked to the polls to exercise their voting privilege as citizens. Tired of a long and costly war, the voters were determined to return the country to peace and stability. The elections were proof that the six-year civil war that cost 3 to 4 million lives through fighting and the resulting humanitarian catastrophe may finally be over. The UN provided unprecedented and much-needed electoral assistance—an estimated 270 million U.S. dollars. While this sounds like a huge sum of money to spend on an election, you must think about the country's geographic conditions.

President Joseph Kabila and his wife, Olive, wave to supporters during a campaign rally shortly before the July 2006 national elections. Kabila was one of 32 presidential candidates to run for office in the election.

Consider, for example, the logistical nightmare of organizing polls where roads do not exist; and election materials had to be shipped by air, down rivers, or even carried on people's heads through the dense tropical rain forest! Amazingly, the Independent Electoral Commission did its job effectively. The election was conducted with relatively few problems. However, in parts of the country, such as the Ituri district, the elections were somewhat difficult to conduct due to ongoing instability. But an election, even if only partially successful, was a much-needed turning point. Will the elections bring peace to eastern DRC, and stop the rape and plundering? Only time will tell.

## COLTAN AND PEACE

You may not have heard of coltan, but you have it in your cell phone, laptop computer, and other electronic devices.

Columbite-tantalite—*coltan* for short—exists in huge quantities in the eastern areas of Congo. When refined, coltan becomes metallic tantalum, a vital element in creating capacitors that are used in cell phones, laptops, pagers, and other electronic devices. According to the UN Security Council, the global demand for coltan is one reason for the ongoing war. Military forces from neighboring Rwanda, Uganda, and Burundi smuggle coltan from the DRC, and use the revenues to support their efforts in the war. Their armies provide protection and security to the individuals and companies extracting the mineral. Coltan mining is hard work, but pays well by Congo standards. While the average Congolese worker makes 10 U.S. dollars a month, a coltan miner can make anywhere from 10 to 50 U.S. dollars a week. The Rwandan Army made an estimated 250 million U.S. dollars over a period of 18 months through the sale of coltan, even though no coltan is mined in Rwanda! Yet, all countries involved in the war deny exploiting Congo's natural resources. Will the global demand for cell phones keep the Congo in war and misery?

## NO HEALTH CARE FOR MANY

Various United Nations estimates suggest that somewhere between 37 to 75 percent of the Congolese population have no access to health care of any kind. The World Health Organization and UNICEF estimate that 350 million U.S. dollars a year is needed to improve Congo's decayed and woefully inadequate health infrastructure. The situation is compounded by the lack of physicians, nurses, medicines, and adequate hospitals and clinics. Clean water and adequate sanitation facilities are lacking throughout most of the country. Few people understand the importance of hygienic practices. For those who do, such basic essentials as soap, detergents, and antiseptics are often unavailable. Many people die each day from preventable diseases, but few hard data are available to document the widespread human suffering. Various agencies assert that only

An inadequate health-care system is one of the Democratic Republic of the Congo's biggest ongoing concerns. Many Congolese don't have access to health care and those that do often cannot pay for treatment. Fortunately, hospitals such as the Medecins Sans Frontieres in Bunia offer treatment to those who are unable to pay, including these children who were injured during clashes between rival ethnic groups.

when peace returns can they begin to hope for a solution to Congo's medical hardships.

"Donor fatigue" is another major concern to the Congolese. Worldwide, there simply are too many needy people, worthwhile causes, and pleas for financial assistance. As a result, many new requests—even from very needy and legitimate sources—fall on deaf ears. People simply are tired of donating to causes that often appear to be little more than an endless and futile drain on resources. The United Nations, for example, sought 121 million U.S. dollars in humanitarian aid for Congo, but received less than 60 percent of that amount. The UN's World Food Program has received food from donors, but lacks the funds to pay for the planes to deliver it. Relief flights to rebel-controlled eastern Congo were halted in July 2005 because of lack of money for fuel and other expenses.

In an unprecedented joint news conference in March 2006, UN High Commissioner for Refugees (UNHCR) António Guterres, World Food Programme (WFP) Executive Director James Morris, and UN Children's Fund (UNICEF) Executive Director Ann M. Veneman pleaded for global support for the DRC. According to them, the message from the Congolese people is "Don't abandon us at this crucial time and risk a return to the bloody nightmare that we lived through for so many years." Will the world answer their call? Sadly, many Congolese wonder whether the world even hears their desperate cries for help.

## CONCLUSION

Perhaps no country in Africa has suffered more at the hands of foreigners than has the Democratic Republic of the Congo. Certainly, none has been abused, raped, and pillaged more frequently and more savagely by foreign powers. Nowhere in Africa did colonialism leave a more damaging or visible scar. As we leave this beautiful, resource-rich, but deeply troubled country, let us remember some important lessons from geography. Location matters. Eastern DRC is chaotic, but conditions are more stable in the western part of the country. Snowcapped mountains around the equator remind us that location influences climate. Ebola, HIV/AIDS, and pneumonic plague remind us that diseases occur in specific places. And frequently they result from interactions between humans and the natural environments in which they live. Chaotic environments of war promote the spread of disease. Historical events such as colonialism have implications for current realities. Possessing vast natural resources does not guarantee national economic wealth; good governance is critical to stability and success. Finally, events in one country have implications for another; no country stands alone. That is why events in the DRC should concern us. Any outbreak of infectious disease in a distant land, for example, can put the entire world at risk.

Salvatore Bulamuzi, a member of the Lendu community of northeastern DRC, lost his parents, two wives, and five children in a recent attack on the town of Bunia. He echoes the desperation of the Congolese people: "I am convinced now . . . that the lives of Congolese people no longer mean anything to anybody. Not to those who kill us like flies, our brothers who help kill us, or those you call the international community. . . . Even God does not listen to our prayers any more and abandons us."

Like Bulamuzi, the people of the Congo continue to wait, hoping to gain more than a change of their country's name, or a new national flag. They wait for change in their lives—one that will bring peace. The children wait, in hope, for help. How long will they have to wait? Can you hear the cries of the children? They, after all, represent the country's future. What will it hold for them, as well as for the Democratic Republic of the Congo?

# Facts at a Glance

## Physical Geography

**Location** Central Africa, northeast of Angola

**Area** Total: 905,585 square miles (2,345,410 square kilometers); land: 875,542 square miles (2,267,600 square kilometers); water: 30,043 square miles (77,810 square kilometers)

**Climate** Tropical; hot and humid in equatorial river basin; cooler and drier in southern highlands; cooler and wetter in eastern highlands; north of equator—wet season (April to October), dry season (December to February); south of equator—wet season (November to March), dry season (April to October)

**Terrain** Vast central basin is a low-lying plateau; mountains in east; also plateaus, savannas, woodlands, tropical rain forest, and volcanoes

**Elevation Extremes** Lowest point is the Atlantic Ocean (sea level); highest point is Pic Marguerite, 16,765 feet (5,110 meters), on Mont Ngaliema

**Land Use** Arable land, 2.86%; permanent crops, 0.47%; other, 96.67% (2005)

**Irrigated Land** 42.5 square miles (110 square kilometers) (2003)

**Natural Hazards** Periodic droughts in south; Congo River floods (seasonal); in the east, in the Great Rift Valley, there are active volcanoes

**Environmental Issues** Poaching threatens wildlife populations; water pollution; deforestation; refugees responsible for significant deforestation, soil erosion, and wildlife poaching; mining of minerals (coltan—a mineral used in creating capacitors, diamonds, and gold) causing environmental damage

## People

**Population** 62,660,551 (July 2006 est.); males, 31,135,984 (2006 est.); females, 31,524,567 (2006 est.)

**Population Density** 21.7 people per square kilometer

**Population Growth Rate** 3.07% (2006 est.)

**Net Migration Rate** 0.23 migrant(s)/1,000 population (2006 est.)

**Fertility Rate** 6.45 children born/woman (2006 est.)

| | |
|---|---|
| **Life Expectancy at Birth** | Total population: 51.46 years; male, 50.01 years; female, 52.94 years (2006 est.) |
| **Median Age** | 16.2 years; male, 16.0 years; female, 16.4 years (2006 est.) |
| **Ethnic Groups** | More than 200 African ethnic groups of which the majority are Bantu; the four largest tribes—Mongo, Luba, Kongo (all Bantu), and the Mangbetu-Azande (Hamitic) make up about 45% of the population |
| **Religions** | Roman Catholic, 50%; Protestant, 20%; Kimbanguist, 10%; Muslim, 10%; other syncretic sects and indigenous beliefs, 10% |
| **Literacy** | (Age 15 and over can read and write) Total population: 65.5%; male, 76.2%; female, 55.1% (2003 est.) |

### Economy

| | |
|---|---|
| **Currency** | Congolese franc (CDF) |
| **GDP Purchasing Power Parity (PPP)** | $40.67 billion (2005 est.) |
| **GDP Per Capita (PPP)** | $700 (2005 est.) |
| **Labor Force** | N/A |
| **Unemployment** | N/A |
| **Labor Force by Occupation** | Agriculture, NA%; industry, NA%; services, NA% |
| **Industries** | Mining (diamonds, copper, zinc), mineral processing, consumer products (including textiles, footwear, cigarettes, processed foods and beverages), cement, commercial ship repair |
| **Exports** | $1.108 billion (2004 est.) |
| **Imports** | $1.319 billion (2004 est.) |
| **Leading Trade Partners** | Exports: Belgium, 38.3%; U.S., 17.9%; China, 11.7%; France, 8%; Finland, 7.8%; Chile, 4.3% (2004). Imports: South Africa, 16.5%; Belgium, 16.1%; France, 9.1%; Zambia, 8.5%; Kenya, 5.7%; Germany, 4.6%; U.S., 4.5%; Cote d'Ivoire, 4.3%; Netherlands, 4.1% (2004) |
| **Export Commodities** | Diamonds, copper, crude oil, coffee, cobalt |
| **Import Commodities** | Foodstuffs, mining and other machinery, transport equipment, fuels |
| **Transportation** | Roadways: 97,560 miles (157,000 kilometers), including 19 miles (30 kilometers) of expressway; Airports: 234— 25 with paved runways (2006); Waterways: 9,321 miles (15,000 kilometers) |

# Facts at a Glance

## Government

| | |
|---|---|
| **Country** | Name Conventional long form: Democratic Republic of the Congo; Conventional short form: none; Local long form: Republique Democratique du Congo; Local short form: none; Former: Congo Free State, Belgian Congo, Congo/Leopoldville, Congo/Kinshasa, Zaire |
| **Capital City** | Kinshasa |
| **Type of Government** | Transitional government |
| **Head of Government** | President Joseph Kabila (since January 26, 2001) |
| **Independence** | June 30, 1960 (from Belgium) |
| **Administrative Divisions** | 10 provinces and 1 city* (ville); Bandundu, Bas-Congo, Equateur, Kasai-Occidental, Kasai-Oriental, Katanga, Kinshasa*, Maniema, Nord-Kivu, Orientale, and Sud-Kivu |

## Communications

| | |
|---|---|
| **TV stations** | 4 (2001) |
| **Phones (including cellular)** | 2,610,600 (2005) |
| **Internet Users** | 50,000 (2002) |

\* Source: CIA-The World Factbook (2006)

| | |
|---|---|
| **2000 B.C.** | Bantus displace indigenous Pygmy population. |
| **A.D. 700** | Bantus and Pygmies live together and begin establishing trade area. |
| **Early 1400s** | Kongo kingdom established. |
| **1500s** | Kongo kingdom establishes strong central government. |
| **1871** | Henry M. Stanley leads expedition to Congo River and Atlantic Ocean. |
| **1875** | Belgian King Leopold II establishes Congo Free State as his own private property. |
| **1884–1885** | Berlin Conference divides Africa among European nations, granting Congo River Basin to King Leopold. |
| **Late 1890s** | British shipping clerk Edmund Morel begins investigation into Belgian abuses in the Congo. |
| **1904** | Morel's report published, uncovering years of corruption in Congo. |
| **1908** | King Leopold turns ownership of Congo Free State over to Belgian government. |
| **1909** | Death of King Leopold. |
| **1908–1950s** | Belgium continues to oppress Congo. |
| **1950s** | Two nationalist movements emerge: Mouvement National Congolais (MNC), led by Patrice Lumumba, and Association des Bakongo (ABAKO), led by Joseph Kasavubu. |
| **1959** | Belgian authorities ban ABAKO meetings and arrest Kasavubu, widespread rioting in Léopoldville (Kinshasa). |
| **1960** | May: Belgian authorities call for independence elections; three political parties emerge: ABAKO, MNC-Lumumba, and Confédération des Associations du Katanga (CONAKAT), led by Moïse Tshombe; June 30: Congo Free State declares independence and becomes Congo Republic under President Joseph Kasavubu and Prime Minister Patrice Lumumba; July: Congolese Army mutinies against Belgian officers; Moïse Tshombe declares Katanga province a separate state, and, after many attacks, Belgians flee the country and Belgium sends in troops to protect Belgian citizens. |
| **1961** | Four groups claim leadership of Congo: Kasavubu and Mobutu in Léopoldville, Lumumba in Stanleyville, Tshombe in Katanga and King Albert Kalonji in Kasai. |

| | |
|---|---|
| **1963** | Lumumba arrested and assassinated; Katanga rebellion ends and Tshombe flees the country, but returns to become prime minister under Kasavubu. |
| **1965** | November 25: Kasavubu overthrown by Joseph Mobutu. |
| **1970** | Mobutu officially elected as president. |
| **1971** | Congo Republic renamed Republic of Zaire. |
| **Mid-1970s** | Mobutu forces European investors out of Zaire and gives their property to his friends and family. |
| **1977** | Severe economic slump forces Mobutu to allow European investors to return to Zaire. |
| **1984** | July 29: Mobutu reelected to office. |
| **1989** | Zaire defaults on international loans. |
| **1990** | Average yearly income less than one-tenth what it was at independence in 1960; foreign aid cut off by World Bank and IMF. |
| **1996** | Mobutu orders Tutsis to leave Zaire; Tutsis rebel; First Congo War begins. |
| **1997** | May 16: Mobutu overthrown; Laurent Kabila named president, country renamed Democratic Republic of the Congo. |
| **1998** | August 2: Second Congo War begins. |
| **1999** | Kabila refuses to hold elections; July 10: cease-fire signed to ostensibly end Second Congo War. |
| **2001** | January 16: Laurent Kabila assassinated; January 20: Joseph Kabila named president. |
| **2003** | Interim government set up by Joseph Kabila. |
| **July 2005** | Military members attack and kill civilians outside Kinshasa, protestors attacked and killed by policemen throughout DRC, humanitarian Pascal Kibembi murdered by rebels. |
| **2005** | August 13: Ten Congolese Tutsis killed in Burundi at a United Nations refugee camp; December 18–19: Elections held to ratify new constitution. |
| **July 2006** | First multiparty democratic elections since 1960. |

Aryeetey-Attoh, S., ed. *Geography of Sub-Saharan Africa* (2/e). Upper Saddle River, N.J.: Pearson Education, 2003.

CIA—The World Factbook. Available online at
*https://www.cia.gov/cia/publications/factbook/geos/cg.html*

Forbath, Peter. *The River Congo.* New York: E. P. Dutton, 1979.

Gyimah-Boadi, E. *Democratic Reform in Africa: The Quality of Progress.* Boulder, Colo.: Lynne Rienner Publishers, 2004.

Macgaffey, Wyatt. *Kongo Political Culture: The Conceptual Challenge of the Particular.* Bloomington: Indiana University Press, 2000.

Oppong, J. R. *Africa South of the Sahara.* Philadelphia: Chelsea House Publishers, 2005.

Weiss, Herbert. *War and Peace in the Democratic Republic of Congo.* Uppsala, Sweden: Herbert Weiss and Nordiska Afrikainstitute, 2000.

# Further Reading

Edgerton, Robert B. *The Troubled Heart of Africa: A History of the Congo.* New York: St. Martin's Press, 2002.

Haskin, Jeanne M. *The Tragic State of Congo: From Decolonization to Dictatorship.* New York: Algora Publishing, 2005.

Hochschild, Adam. *King Leopold's Ghost: A Story of Greed, Terror and Heroism.* New York: Pan Macmillan, 2006.

O'Hanlon, Redmond. *Congo Journey.* New York: Penguin, 1997.

Taylor, Jeffrey. *Facing the Congo: A Modern-Day Journey into the Heart of Darkness.* New York: Three Rivers Press, 2001.

## Web sites

CIA World Factbook—Democratic Republic of the Congo
*https://www.cia.gov/cia/publications/factbook/geos/cg.html*

Congo Nature and Culture
*www.congo2005.be*

Congo Pages
*www.congo-pages.org/*

Wikipedia
*http://en.wikipedia.org/wiki/Democratic_Republic_of_the_Congo*

The Democratic Republic of the Congo
*http://www.globalissues.org/Geopolitics/Africa/DRC.asp*

Human Rights Watch
*http://hrw.org/doc/?t=africa&c=congo*

DRC on the Internet
*http://library.stanford.edu/africa/zaire.html*

National Geographic Congo Trek
*http://www.nationalgeographic.com/congotrek/*

PBS Congo Rain Forest
*http://www.pbs.org/wnet/africa/explore/rainforest/rainforest_resources.html*

Baka Pygmies of the Congo
*http://www.pygmies.info/*

U.S. Department of State, Congo (Kinshasa) Page
*www.state.gov/r/pa/ei/bgn/2823.htm*

UNESCO—Protecting the Treasures of the Democratic Republic of the Congo
*www.unesco.org/dossiers/congo*

United Nations Mission of Democratic Republic of Congo
*http://www.un.int/drcongo/*

World Conservation Society
*http://www.wcs.org/international/Africa/drcongo*

# Index

AIDS, 14, 31, 46, 50, 75–76
Albert, Lake, 20, 27
Alliance of Democratic Forces for the
    Liberation of Congo-Zaire
    (ADFL), 67–68
animals, 13, 27–29, 30
Association des Bakongo (ABAKO),
    39–40

Bambuti tribe, 58–59
Bantu tribes, 32, 34
Banyamulenge, 68
Bas-Zaïre region, logging in, 30
Belgium, 13–14, 35–39, 41
Bemba, Jean-Pierre, 70, 72
Berlin Conference, 35, 36
biodiversity, 28, 29–31
bonobos, 28, 29
bribery, 55–56
Bulamuzi, Salvatore, 89
Bunia, attack on, 89
bushmeat, 30

cannibalism, 75
cassava, 47–48, 54
centrifugal and centripetal forces, lan-
    guage and, 11
children, 14, 24, 50–51, 57, 77–78
cholera, 76
Christianity, 56–57
climate and weather, overview of,
    20–22
colonialism, paternalistic, 39
coltan, 80, 85–86
commerce, women and, 49–50
Confédération des Associations du
    Katanga (CONAKAT), 40
Congo Free State, King Leopold and,
    35–38
Congo River, 22, 23, 33, 43, 62
Congo River Basin region, 18, 19, 21
Congolese Army, 70
cultural diffusion, 45–46
cultural geography, 15

culture, spread of, 45–48
curfews, 39
currency, Joseph Mobutu and, 65

daily life, overview of, 52–54
dashes, 55–56
diamonds, 64, 80
diffusion, 45–48
diseases, 14, 30, 75–77, 86
diversity, instability and, 11
Djibouti, Great Rift Valley and, 27
Doctors Without Borders, 87
donor fatigue, 87–88

earthquakes, 23, 81
Eastern Highlands region, 18–20
Ebola, 30–31, 76
education, 41, 50, 52, 70–71, 74
elderly, role of in society, 51
elections, 70–71, 82, 84–85
elephants, 35
elevation, 17–18, 21
Elisabethville, 43
Emmanuelle (child soldier), 78
energy reserves, 13
environmental issues, 13, 29–31
equatorial location, influence of, 21
Eritrea, Great Rift Valley and, 27
ethnic violence, 74–75, 79
Europe, 34–39
expansion diffusion, 45–48
Eyskens, Gaston, 42

faulting, Great Rift Valley and, 26–27
fauna, 13, 27–29
ferries, 62, 63
fighting, 14, 55. *See also* wars
First Congo War, 65–66
fishing, Wagenia people and, 16
fleeing, survival and, 56
flora, 27–28
food, 47–48, 61
Force Publique, 37
forced labor, 35–37

**JOSEPH R. OPPONG** is associate professor of geography at the University of North Texas in Denton and a native of Ghana. He has nearly two decades of university teaching experience in Ghana, Canada, and the United States. His research focuses on medical geography—the geography of disease and health care. This is his fourth Chelsea House book.

**TANIA WOODRUFF** is a senior at the University of North Texas, where she is majoring in geography. Her hobbies include reading, writing, and playing with her daughter. When she graduates, she plans to work for a nonprofit organization bringing relief to poverty-stricken nations.

**CHARLES F. GRITZNER** is distinguished professor of geography at South Dakota State University in Brookings. He is now in his fifth decade of college teaching, research, and writing. In addition to teaching, he enjoys writing, working with teachers, and sharing his love of geography with readers. As series editor for the MODERN WORLD CULTURES and MODERN WORLD NATIONS series, he has a wonderful opportunity to combine each of these hobbies. Gritzner has served as both president and executive director of the National Council for Geographic Education. He also has received many national honors, including the George J. Miller Award for Distinguished Service to Geographic Education from the NCGE, the Association of American Geographers Gilbert Grosvenor Honors in Geography Education, and Distinguished Teaching Achievements awards from the Association of American Geographers.